1994

Consequences of the Clinton Victory

Essays on the First Year

Consequences of the Clinton Victory

Essays on the First Year

Peter W. Schramm
editor

Ashbrook Press
Ashland, Ohio

ISBN 1-878802-18-6

Ashbrook Press

Publisher for the
John M. Ashbrook Center for Public Affairs
Ashland University
Ashland, Ohio 44805
(419) 289-5411

Printed in the United States of America

dedicated to the memory of

Thomas A. Van Meter

Table of Contents

Introduction

This volume appears exactly one year after Bill Clinton took office as the 42nd President of the United States. The reader may rightly ask what justifies our quick analysis? After all, it certainly can be argued that whatever the Clinton presidency does, and the manner in which it ends up accounting for itself, will not be fully clear until the end of his term, if then. But while many details will be added to the story during the next three years, the nature of Mr. Clinton's campaign and his first year in office is such that citizens are justified in coming to some solid conclusions now about the new regime and its purposes.

No one was surprised that this presidency did not have a honeymoon period, or that none was requested. Mr. Clinton's theme during the campaign was change, and he invited us to scrutinize him from the first days on. He encouraged us to expect immediate change; the executive-legislative gridlock would be broken. He claimed that this dreaded gridlock had stymied the nation for twelve years, and that he was more than ready to get the country moving again as soon as he was in the driver's seat. We were led to believe that once the deadlock was over, as a matter of fact and political affiliation, the federal government would once again become the well-oiled machine some think it should always be and the nation would be on the move again. The consequence of his victory would be fast change, a swift attack on the many ills of our society, with the full cooperation of the Democrats in Congress.

This is not to say, however, that the new president had a mandate for change. He was elected with only 43 percent of the national vote, having won a majority of the votes in only two states (Arkansas gave him 53.7 percent while New York allowed him 50.1 percent.) Further, he won a smaller percentage of the votes in their respective states than did all Democratic senators elected in 1992 and all but four House Democrats in their districts. He couldn't very well contend that he had a mandate, national or local, and certainly could not argue that victorious Democratic Congressmen came in on his coattails.

Added to these facts was the aggravation of the Democratic losses in important state and local elections during Mr. Clinton's first year. The Democrats lost the U.S. Senate runoff election in Georgia; they lost the special Senate election in Texas; they lost governors' races in Virginia and New Jersey, and a lieutenant governor's race in Arkansas; and for the first time in a generation Republicans were elected as mayors of Los Angeles and New York. The meaning of these losses was obvious to all, and admitted by the candid. These convulsions in the body politic showed that voters had reconsidered their earlier, if limited, enthusiasm for the Democrats. Stated less charitably, they were manifestations of the people's doubt about Clinton's capacities to govern. Because of his attempt at a perpetual campaign, and the many blunders of the first six months, some began to think that he was a small man living in a large house and that he was there only by mishap.

Although he did not receive a ringing mandate, the new president grabbed the steering wheel of the government firmly. On the night of his election victory he said: "This election is a clarion call for our country to face the challenges of the end of the Cold War and the beginning of the next century." He added, even more philosophically: "We need more than new laws, new promises or new programs. We need a new spirit of community, a sense that we're all in this together." After the vote Clinton continued to refer to his theme of change. He was the head of the clean-up crew that would sweep out the philosophy and policies of the selfish, all-too-awful twelve years of Reaganism. Even after the campaign was over he continued to show the utmost contempt and even ridicule of those Republican years. He was certain that his time had come.

Some argued that the new president was an old liberal anxious to add more horse power to the machine built by Franklin D. Roosevelt. But Mr. Clinton claimed to be an entirely new Democrat. His association with the Democratic Leadership Council was useful; the DLC was interested in Democrats winning elections by applying conservative means to liberal ends. Clinton seemed to have clearer purposes and a more effervescent attitude than his most recent Democratic predecessors had when they ran unsuccessfully for the same office. Since this was a new model Democrat, he didn't have Democratic heroes to whom he could (publicly) appeal in matters of substance—except perhaps Jefferson, although that seemed contrived—and perhaps that explains his many favorable references to Lincoln. But Clinton clearly had a hero in matters of style and character: John F. Kennedy. His emphasis on the new generation taking charge clearly alluded to the Kennedy myth of dynamism and change harkening to the future. But upon closer examination it became increasingly obvious that he was by no means disowning the liberal vision of the large bureaucratic state, with its many entitlement programs.

This Democrat *sui generis* would emphasize economic growth rather than redistribution of the wealth that had already been created by the rational and the industrious. Although he would increase the taxes on the very rich (who had so selfishly profited during the bad years) he would not do so on the middle class, whom he was keen on representing and benefitting. He would also reduce the deficit and the debt, and still increase spending on new programs. He would create more and better jobs. He was for free trade and in an artful way tied together his domestic agenda for change with the newly competitive international environment. He was also deeply concerned about everyone's security and health, as well as that of the environment, and thereby revealed to all that he was a caring leader who knew the true basis of community. He said that the military should remain strong and, despite his personal history, indicated that he would be willing to use it—in Bosnia, for example, where he accused Bush of being fainthearted. He would attack the problem of welfare by explaining that the recipients of government largess also had obligations to the good hearted community of which they are a part. He would overcome the problem of racial divisiveness by replicating the appearance of America in his cabinet through group representation.

Much has been said about Clinton (and Gore) being of the sixties generation, and it is true that his personal philosophy seems to have been deeply affected by the sixties' transvaluation of values. His health care proposal and his wife's pleas for a "politics of meaning" perhaps most clearly reveal the connection between New Deal liberalism and sixties radicalism. He would do nothing less than reinvent government, if not human nature itself. He would practice a kind of politics of joy and a politics of good intentions that would be mystically elevated into the politics of meaning.

That Clinton's first six months in office were nearly catastrophic may be a reflection of both fundamental problems in his ends and means, and his inability to please the various hungry factions within the Democratic Party. His artful tergiversations on a number of issues—not excluding taxes, family values, and foreign policy—may be nothing more than a clear indication that this president is a willing learner. (We are reminded that it took Jimmy Carter three years of being president before he came to realize, by his own admission, the true nature of Soviet communism.) On the other hand, they may be signals that reflect on his political insubstantiality and inconstancy, that he may be no surer—to use Coriolanus' estimate of the Roman people—"than is the coal of fire upon the ice, or hailstone in the sun." Either way, the self-absorbed factions within the Democratic party—from the homosexual lobby to the DLC to the labor unions—are in a spirited mood, and the president cannot ignore their demands without paying a heavy price. The consequences of the Clinton victory are becoming manifest, and those of us interested in tactical and strategic skirmishes will have a lot to look forward to; the next three years of his administration will not be sound and fury signifying nothing. May we live in interesting times!

The fourteen essays in this volume argue that many of the core elements of the Clinton regime have been revealed, and that we can begin to see the consequences of this new kind of politics. Although critical, they take the Clinton phenomenon in American politics seriously. They give the president credit for his intelligence and determination. No one underestimates his abilities, or doubts the seriousness of his purposes. His speeches and actions are taken as they are offered. There is an attempt to put them in a historical context, as well as to offer the necessary theoretical interpretation of their essence.

Our authors seek to shed light on the meaning of the Clinton presidency for the sake of illuminating the deliberations and choices facing the citizens of America. In this way we hope to be of use to our fellow citizens on whose capacity for self-government the future of the Republic depends.

December 8, 1993   Peter W. Schramm
Ashland, Ohio

Clinton's First Year

William A. Rusher

Any evaluation of the first year of the Clinton presidency must begin with an appreciation of how Mr. Clinton came to be elected in the first place.

Some presidents—Ronald Reagan comes to mind—are swept into office on the crest of some powerful new impulse in the body politic. Others (George Bush, for example) are elected precisely because the voters are satisfied with the status quo and want as little change as possible. Finally there are those, such as Jimmy Carter, who are chosen, not because they stand for anything the voters especially want, but simply because their opponents are marginally less appealing. Bill Clinton's victory, with just 43 percent of the popular vote, clearly falls into the latter category.

President Bush's high approval ratings after the Gulf War had the effect of persuading all of the best-known and most formidable Democratic possibilities—Bradley, Cuomo, Gephardt, Gore, and Rockefeller—to sit out 1992 and wait for 1996. That left the race for the 1992 Democratic nomination to the "B team": Brown, Clinton, Harkin, Kerrey, and Tsongas.

This was the uninspiring litter of which Mr. Clinton turned out to be the pick.

But no sooner had Clinton nailed down the nomination than Bush began a slide in the polls which continued right through election day. The reason is no mystery: He fatally disregarded the growing public perception that the country was in a depression. Subsequent analyses suggest that the perception was false, but it was certainly real. The "chattering classes," in particular, were suffering economically, and made sure that everyone knew it. Yet Mr. Bush repeatedly allowed himself to be photographed in his golf cart and on his speedboat, gamely insisting that there was no recession and urging everyone to wait for his (thoroughly forgettable) acceptance speech at the Republican convention.

The situation was rendered vastly more complicated by the entry, withdrawal, and reentry of Ross Perot into the race as an independent candidate. Tapping into widespread public concern over the annual federal deficits, and even more general public disgust with the professional politicians of both parties, Perot managed to win 19 percent of the voters on election day. A large majority of these had voted twice for Reagan and then for Bush. Clinton's 43 percent was almost identical to the vote rolled up by Dukakis in 1988.

But not even that 43 percent represented a bloc of voters determinedly loyal to Clinton. Among them, it seems clear, were millions who doubted his truthfulness, and more generally his character, but who simply could not bring themselves to vote for four more years of George Bush or run the unknowable risks of a Perot presidency.

To be sure, the fact that both houses of Congress are controlled by his party represents a plus that no Republican in the White House has enjoyed since the first term of Dwight

Eisenhower. But the longstanding division of power between Democratic Congresses and Republican presidents has led the Democrats to create almost a "shadow government" at the eastern end of Pennsylvania Avenue: the staffs of Congressional committees and other organizations (such as the Congressional Budget Office) that closely monitor every act of the executive departments and agencies. It became clear that these were not going to fold up merely because a Democrat had been elected president.

President Clinton's Cabinet appointments reflected his declared wish for a Cabinet that would "look more like America." It certainly contains a little bit of everything—a black, a Hispanic, several women, etc.—but its apparent catholicity was diminished considerably when somebody pointed out that it contains more millionaires than Mr. Bush's.

Unfortunately one of its weakest members appears right at the top of the list: Warren Christopher, a California attorney whose work as chair of the committee to review vice presidential possibilities so impressed Mr. Clinton that he made him his Secretary of State. In view of Clinton's own unfamiliarity with foreign affairs, and his famous lack of interest in the subject, it was crucial that he have a strong Secretary of State.

Instead, Christopher has already acquired such a reputation for inadequacy that public calls for his resignation have come from a prominent Democratic Congressman and London's respected weekly, *The Economist*, among others.

The new president's early months in the White House revealed, moreover, a dismaying clumsiness. Mostly because he held the press at arm's length before his inauguration, he never had to explain how Johnetta Cole, a radical friend of Ms. Rodham Clinton's with ties to the notorious pro-Castro Venceremos Brigade and other Communist-affiliated organizations, happened to be appointed to a high post in his transition team. But the Clinton's close personal friends Harry Thomason and his wife Linda Bloodsworth-Thomason were rashly given the run of the White House, and were soon caught trying to toss the lucrative business of its travel office to friends.

Clinton's first nominee for the post of Attorney General, Zoe Baird, was compelled to step down when it was discovered, belatedly, that she had violated the Tax and Immigration laws. A similar fate overtook the next choice for that post, Judge Kimba Wood, even though she was apparently not guilty of the particular offense that had felled Ms. Baird. Lani Guinier, whose father was secretary-treasurer of a union expelled from the CIO because it was Communist-controlled, had to withdraw as Mr. Clinton's nominee for the post of Assistant Attorney General for Civil Rights when the president finally got around to reading what she had written.

As for serious matters of policy, Mr. Clinton abandoned, even before he was inaugurated, his pledge not to raise taxes on the middle class, offering the traditional excuse that he hadn't discovered until after the election how big the deficit was. Unfortunately for this explanation, Mr. Clinton had repeatedly insisted, during the campaign, that the actual deficit was just as big as he ultimately "discovered" it to be. At the same time, and most foolishly, he insisted on pushing ahead with his plan to order the admission of avowed homosexuals to the armed forces—a step which he had declared, during the campaign, could be accomplished "with a stroke of a pen." Instead, he wound up being forced by Senator Nunn and an uncooperative Congress into a humiliating backdown in which the regulations against open homosexuality in the military were not only reaffirmed but, for the first time, written into statute law.

Many of these blunders could have been avoided if the Clinton team had simply been more experienced in the ways of the White House. No doubt the appointment of David Gergen, the former Nixon and Reagan advisor, to a high post in charge of making the president look better will have a beneficial effect. Indeed, it is already doing so: There have been no more traffic-stopping $200 haircuts on the runway at Los Angeles International Airport, nor are there likely to be.

But in the nature of things not even Gergen can shield Mr. Clinton from the effects of his often bruising encounters with Congress, let alone from the visibly disastrous consequences of his foreign policies.

Clinton's first major clash with Congress was painful but at least educational. Putting his "stimulus package" before the lawmakers, he calculated that the Democratic majorities would stand by him, and decided to simply shove the package down the Republicans' throats. That gave the Republicans a superb opportunity to depict themselves as the foes of higher taxes: Every single Republican in the House of Representatives voted against the bill. Mr. Clinton duly mowed them down, but then discovered to his horror that 40 senators can filibuster a bill to death—and there were 43 Republicans in the Senate! Under the brilliant leadership of minority leader Bob Dole, they opposed the stimulus package unanimously and launched a filibuster. End of package.

Mr. Clinton apparently learned from that experience, because he fought hard, and in the end more successfully, for his budget bill. But so many Democrats defected in the Senate that Vice President Gore had to break a tie, and the measure passed by a single vote in the House, after wavering Democrats had been promised everything but the Capital dome.

Congressional ratification of NAFTA was universally hailed as a victory for Mr. Clinton, and indeed it was, if one recalls how hard he worked (and how liberally he deployed the powers of the presidency) to secure its passage. But the agreement's comfortable margin in the House (234 to 200) looks distinctly less comfortable when one remembers that 132 of those 234 votes were cast by Republicans. The Congressmen of Mr. Clinton's own party voted heavily against him—156 to 102—on this major bill, on which he had gambled everything he had.

These are not results that a new president in his first year can point to with much pride. The Congressional Democrats have clearly taken Mr. Clinton's measure, and are not in the least afraid of him.

In the extremely important matter of Supreme Court appointments, on the other hand, Mr. Clinton has had just one opportunity to name a justice, and he handled it rather adroitly. In nominating Ruth Bader Ginsburg, he chose a firm liberal whose judicial skills, as already displayed on the District of Columbia Circuit, are known to have impressed both Justice Antonin Scalia, the Supreme Court's leading conservative, and Senator Orrin Hatch, the ranking Republican on the Senate Judiciary Committee. Add to this the fact that she is a woman and the first Jew to sit on the Court since Abe Fortas, Mr. Clinton can be congratulated on an appointment that was judicially defensible and politically shrewd.

There is one other area in which the Clinton administration has similarly exceeded expectations, at least thus far. The president's wife, Hillary Rodham Clinton, is obviously a highly intelligent woman with many ideas on what government needs to accomplish and a firm determination to help the process. She has, moreover, her husband's enthusiastic consent to her participation in the active work of his administration. When she accepted the assignment of drafting the president's health care proposal, it was widely expected that she had bitten off more than she could chew, and that her aggressive style would alienate many voters.

Thus far, however, it hasn't turned out that way. Ms. Rodham Clinton's approval rating in national polls is well ahead of her husband's. She managed to bring the health plan through its lengthy birth agonies, while still striking most people as bright, good-natured, and resourceful. Just recently, as critics of her plan started weighing in with their objections, she has begun to show an edge of exasperation that does not become her and which, if continued, may start offending people (calling some of the criticisms "lies," for example). But up to now, it is fair to say, she has proved a bigger asset to her husband than many of their opponents had anticipated.

In the field of defense, Mr. Clinton's own notoriously anti-military inclinations have been modified, not only by the exigencies of his new responsibilities as commander in chief, but by the counsel of his relatively moderate Secretary of Defense, former Congressman Les Aspin. The Clinton reductions in the military budget are in many cases not all that much greater than those proposed by President Bush. Recently Aspin has come under criticism for various derelictions, from refusing to send tanks to Somalia to lacking any clear concept of a military policy for Haiti. But in an administration bulging with leftists he remains, at least relatively, an influence for common sense.

It is in foreign affairs that Mr. Clinton's performance thus far has proved most ominous. His defenders argue, with justice, that he deserves credit for having stuck by Boris Yeltsin at various points when the Russian leader, and with him the hope of a democratic and market-oriented Russia, were in great peril. He also managed to avoid doing anything visibly wrong at the G-7 summit in Tokyo. But, with those exceptions, his record in the foreign arena has been one long succession of missteps and failures, several of them serious enough to be called disasters.

Having criticized President Bush during the campaign for not doing enough to block Serbian aggression in Bosnia, Clinton sent Secretary of State Christopher to Europe to round up support for the lifting of sanctions and the launching of air strikes. But the Europeans, like the Congressional Democrats, have sized Mr. Clinton up as a paper tiger, and Secretary Christopher similarly failed to impress them. He came home empty-handed, and Mr. Clinton settled for blaming our European allies for making it impossible for him to do anything.

On the subject of Haiti, too, Clinton had been a sharp critic of the Bush policy, and had vowed to stop turning back refugees from that tormented island. But once in office he quickly—and, let it be said, wisely—reversed himself. He also, much less wisely, sought to impose the elected president, an unstable and pro-Communist ex-priest, Jean Bertrand Aristede, on a reluctant military, and wound up making the United States look ridiculous when its soldiers, sent to Port-au-Prince with inadequate arms, had to sail away without landing when threatened by rioters onshore.

Even in Somalia, where the Bush administration had committed American forces to insure the delivery of food and humanitarian supplies, Mr. Clinton allowed himself to be talked by UN Secretary General Boutros Boutros-Ghali into turning the operation into an ambitious "peace-making" expedition to build a new government, and thence into a preposterous search-and-destroy mission with a cash reward for the capture (never achieved) of an uncooperative local warlord.

Only in the Middle East has the situation improved during Mr. Clinton's first year in office, and there, significantly, progress was made where the administration had least to do with it and knew least about it. The Israelis and the PLO reached agreement in secret talks in Oslo, under the sponsorship of the Norwegian foreign minister. Subsequently Israeli foreign minister Peres traveled all the way to Santa Barbara to notify Secretary Christopher, who was vacationing there.

Approaching the end of his first year as president, therefore, Mr. Clinton has, as Winston Churchill once acidly remarked of Clement Attlee, a great deal to be modest about. But he clearly believes that his health care proposal, now beginning its long journey through the legislative process, may yet earn him a place among the presidents memorable for their great achievements. The readiness to compromise on health care that he has already displayed—almost everything, it seems, is negotiable except that it must be universal—suggests that his ultimate goal is political: Whatever Congress passes next year, he evidently reasons, he can claim paternity and be hailed forever afterward as "the president who brought universal health care to America."

But it is, of course, precisely this accolade that his opponents will seek to deny him. The bill as ultimately passed will not only bear little resemblance to the one submitted by him and his energetic wife; it may well be named (quite accurately) "the Jones-Brown Act" or whatever, in honor of its Congressional authors. Getting the credit for it may not prove as easy as Mr. Clinton expects.

On the evidence of his first year, in any case, it is not only Rush Limbaugh who finds Mr. Clinton seriously lacking. During 1992 it seemed possible that he might indeed prove to be the kind of "new Democrat" he professed to be: ready to acknowledge that the old liberal nostrums had failed, and to work with such creative forces in his own party as the Democratic Leadership Council (which he once chaired) to find new solutions for the nation's problems. But once in the Oval Office he quickly sidelined relatively moderate Democrats, repudiated his own pledge not to raise taxes, cynically scuttled the Hatch Act (which had kept federal employees out of political campaigns), signed a bill enabling welfare recipients to register to vote while picking up their checks, and revived the old politics of envy with the clearest appeal to class warfare since the early days of the New Deal.

The public has responded by giving his performance the poorest rating, at this point in his term, of any president since the polls began.

And yet it is much too early to dismiss Bill Clinton as doomed to be a one-term president. If the economy manages to emerge from its long doldrums, despite the burdensome new taxes and other obligations that Mr. Clinton seems bent on imposing on its job-producing sectors, he will be given credit for the fact that people are "better off now than they were four years ago." And if Ross Perot decides to enter the presidential race again, he may, even though no longer able to command 19 percent of the votes, deprive the Republican candidate of just enough of them to reelect Mr. Clinton.

For after all, as Richard Nixon demonstrated long ago, a candidate does not have to persuade the voters to love him, but only to find him marginally more acceptable (or less offensive) than his rivals. Mr. Clinton succeeded in doing exactly that in 1992, and it would be rash indeed to conclude, just yet, that he won't be able to do it again in 1996.

— 2 —

The Reagan Legacy
and Liberal Opportunities

Thomas B. Silver

The defeat of the incumbent president in the '92 elections, after a three man race, left the Democrats looking forward jubilantly to only the second Democratic administration since the Republican domination of the presidency began way back in the '60s. The president-elect, a man of some resilience and resourcefulness, had survived partisan taunts of sexual misconduct and draft-dodging on his way to the White House. His victory was made possible, in no small part, by a bill signed by the Republican president in October of '90 that significantly increased the nation's tax burden and that was followed, weeks later, by his party's defeat in the Congressional elections. The new president would take office amidst a sharp national debate over both foreign and domestic policy. In foreign policy, the nation was struggling to define its role in a world where the United States had no enemy that could pose an immediate threat to its survival and security. In domestic policy the great question was whether a new era was at hand in which a significant expansion of federal authority was needed to curb the excesses of the rich and the ambitions of powerful corporate raiders and empire builders.

I speak here of the election of 1892, in which Grover Cleveland returned the Democracy to power, riding on a wave of resentment against Republican economic policies. As a Reaganite, my purpose in drawing a parallel between 1892 and 1992 is not to make the reassuring point that the Republicans recaptured the presidency in 1896 and went on to win six of the next eight presidential elections. My purpose, on the contrary, is the more disquieting one of arguing that in 1992, as in 1892, we are at the end of an era in American political history and that it may be a new progressive impulse, rather than the conservatism of Ronald Reagan, that carries us into the twenty-first century.

The argument, more specifically, is that a quarter century of economic/financial instability may now be drawing to a close, just as it did in the 1890s, at the same moment when the most resonant issue for Republican orators (the threat of communism) has now gone the way of the bloody shirt. The closure of these issues in the 1890s, together with the rise of the great financiers and corporate raiders of the 1880s, opened the door to the Progressive Era.[1] To the extent that something similar is happening today, Ronald Reagan and Bill Clinton may be, respectively, the omega and the alpha of two distinct periods of American history.

This conclusion is reinforced by the fact, as we now know, that 1980 was not a "critical election" wherein one party breaks the back of the other and dictates the political agenda for a generation. Reagan passed up the opportunity to declare an economic emergency in 1981, and he refused for eight years to draw a line in the sand against the Democrats in Congress. By rejecting the high risk strategy of forcing the main enemy forces into a conclusive battle, Reagan settled for a policy of incremental successes that would always be exposed to counterattack by the unbloodied and uncowed liberal Democratic majority in Congress.

The Progressive Era (which I define arbitrarily for this article as the time between Grover Cleveland and Warren Harding) had this interesting feature: it contained no critical elections and yet it brought to the fore explicitly the kind of "regime" questions that are at the heart of critical elections. It was not until 1932 that the intellectual core of Progressive thought reached its full political incarnation. I believe that we may now be entering into another such era of American history, and I also believe that the phenomenon of Bill Clinton must be taken with the utmost seriousness, and not regarded simply as a transient reaction to the failures of George Bush.

THE REAGAN PRESIDENCY: DO AS I SAY, NOT AS I DO

Ronald Reagan was a giant of an economic statesman, in comparison with his immediate predecessor and his immediate successor, just as a man of average height is a giant in comparison with midgets. Economic growth in the 1980s was about the same as the postwar average achieved by Presidents Truman through Carter. Inflation was much better than it was under Ford/Carter, much worse than it was under Eisenhower/Kennedy. One reason for this mediocre record was that Reagan's speeches and deeds went together like a pair of mismatched socks.

In fiscal policy, Reagan spoke loudly and carried a small stick. His 1981 tax cuts were a bold departure from Republican orthodoxy of the past half century, but were significantly watered down by tax increases in 1982, 1984 and 1986. One remembers his soaring rhetoric in 1980 about the need to liberate the entrepreneurial spirit of America, yet one also cannot forget the sobering reality of his 40 percent increase in the capital gains tax in 1986.[2] For decades the federal tax burden as a fraction of gross national product has averaged between 19 percent and 20 percent. In 1980 it was a little over 19 percent; in 1990 it was a little over 19 percent. The decade of the eighties may have been many things, but when it comes to tax policy it was certainly not a revolution.

What of federal spending under Reagan? Again, rhetoric and reality went their separate ways. When Reagan took office, federal spending was over 22 percent of gross national product. His first OMB report projected that spending would decline to 19.3 percent of GNP by 1984! That was the rhetoric. The reality was that spending as a proportion of GNP when Reagan left office stood at 22.3 percent of GNP—just about where it was on the day he entered the Oval Office. The fiscal debaters in Washington during the 1980s were like a bunch of little boys playing marbles on the playground: the noise they made and the passsions they felt were far out of proportion to the actual stakes of the game.

It is not a persuasive defense of Reagan to say that he did the best he could given a spendthrift Congress. In the first place, there was not a huge difference between what he requested and what he got, especially in an economy the size of ours. For example, in 1985 Reagan's budget requested federal outlays of $940 billion and the actual outlays were $946 billion. The difference is chicken feed. Second, Reagan never used his veto power to any great extent. Finally, he never used the power of Gramm-Rudman, which was the practical equivalent of the balanced budget amendment to the Constitution.

Reagan's monetary policy was an even greater disappointment. For most of his presidency it bore no resemblance whatsoever to the policy he campaigned on and made a pillar of his 1981 economic program. Reagan, an economics major at Eureka College, was something of a student of monetary policy, a classical liberal, a follower of Ludwig Von Mises and Milton Friedman. As such, he had a long and deeply held belief in the following propositions. First, when it comes to inflation and recession, government is the problem; specifically, government's monetary policy is the problem. Second, politicians cause inflation when they "print" money to lower interest rates and stimulate the economy artificially. This shortsighted policy is successful at first, but after a while, inflation and interest rates start to rise. In order to avoid runaway inflation, the political authorities are compelled to reduce the printing of money, which raises interest rates and slows the economy. In a nutshell, the benefits of excessive monetary growth are transient and ephemeral; in the longer run, we are left with the twin evils of inflation and the business cycle, i.e., periodic recessions. Third, the proper monetary policy would entail the slow, steady, growth of money that is characterized by a gold standard or a fiat money policy that mimics the gold standard ("monetarism").[3] Money growth needs to be slow to eliminate or minimize inflation; it needs to be steady to eliminate or moderate recessions. Since inflation and recessions cause distortions in the allocation of resources, slow, steady growth of the money supply is the sine qua non for sustained growth at peak efficiency.[4]

In accordance with these propositions, Reagan's 1981 economic recovery program called for a gradual but persistent reduction of money growth over several years to wring inflation out of the economy without wringing the economy's neck. Unfortunately, the exact opposite happened. A few months into Reagan's first term, the Federal Reserve slammed on the monetary brakes and the economy went through the windshield. The 1981-1982 recession was the most devastating downturn since the thirties. So much for gradualism![5]

A year later, the Fed took its foot off the brake and jammed the accelerator pedal to the floor. The economy took off on "the longest peacetime expansion in American history." So much for steadiness!

Year after year, new money gushed out of the Federal Reserve's printing presses without a murmur of protest from Milton Friedman's student, Ronald Reagan. Indeed, the president reappointed Paul Volcker as chairman of the Fed, thereby stamping his imprimatur on Jimmy Carter's choice for the job. Each year from 1983 through 1986, growth of M-2 surpassed the M-2 growth in the years 1977-1980.

ANNUAL PERCENT GROWTH OF M-2

Carter		Reagan	
1977	10.6	1983	12.0
1978	7.9	1984	8.6
1979	7.8	1985	8.2
1980	8.9	1986	9.4

It was as though Ronald Reagan, having criticized Carter for adding a swing shift to the Fed's printing presses, himself added a graveyard shift so that the Fed could print money non-stop, 24 hours a day. So much for slow money growth! The sad fact is that Ronald Reagan's monetary policy was not gradual; it was not slow; it was not steady. In a word, it was not Reaganomics.

The steep economic nosedive in 1982 had one positive result. It brought inflation down from double digits to just under four per cent. This, however, was not the same as "breaking the back" of inflation. Four per cent, after all, was the level of inflation that had frightened Richard Nixon just a decade before into imposing wage and price controls, with the enthusiastic approval of the country. (In the century following the American Civil War, inflation had averaged about one per cent per annum.) In any event, as the recovery went on, four per cent gave way to five per cent and then six per cent inflation in response to the relentless money growth under Reagan.

This was not a brilliant record, but there is another side to the story that reflects more credit on Ronald Reagan and that may have profound implications for the future of American politics.

THE CASE FOR REAGAN: HE KEPT US OUT OF EVEN DEEPER VOODOO

Among American presidents, Ronald Reagan is the most impressive economic leader certainly of the past generation and perhaps the past two generations. This is not because in the kingdom of the blind the one-eyed man is king, for actually he was remarkably clear-sighted. What he lacked at times was the hardness or ruthlessness required for a thoroughgoing implementation of Reaganomics—a ruthlessness that would have exposed him to greater political risk and at worst may have been no more successful than what he did achieve, given the unholy alliance in Congress between insatiable special interests on the one hand and invincible ignorance on the other.

It is true that after Reagan's initial tax cut, the federal tax burden rose throughout his second term. In fairness, however, it must be pointed out that it never reached the peak (20 percent of GNP) that it did under President Carter. Spending, meanwhile, having peaked after (and because of) the 1982 recession at 24 percent of GNP, declined sharply in Reagan's second term, largely because Reagan was having some success in containing domestic spending. A dramatic proof of this is to compare domestic spending for 1985 in constant (1991) dollars with domestic spending for 1989 in constant (1991) dollars: $684.3 billion vs. $689.3 billion. In other words, real domestic spending was virtually flat during Reagan's second term.[6]

When Reagan's presidency is measured, not by his rhetoric, but simply on the basis of what he inherited from Jimmy Carter and what he bequeathed to George Bush, it must be judged a success. From this point of view, Bush's presidency can only be regarded—to draw upon the sports metaphors of which he was so fond—as a blown save. Apart from monetary policy, where he kept faith with Mr. Reagan by reappointing Alan Greenspan (about which more later), Bush's economic program seemed to be designed as a massive rebuke to voodoo economics. Even if one excuses his signature on far reaching regulatory legislation such as the Clean Air Act and the Americans With Disabilities Act, as the shrewd counsel of political expediency—after all, how many Republicans in Congress voted against them?[7]—what can one possibly say about his fiscal policies? With respect to the tax increase, even Bush now realizes that he should have read his own lips instead of Richard Darman's.

Domestic spending under Bush burst the bonds in which Reagan had confined it. Hell, it burst the bonds in which Carter had confined it. Under Carter, domestic spending increased 12 percent over four years; under Bush a whopping 24 percent.

Obviously, much of this is attributable to the recession, but even Bush's post-recession budget projections did not show that the spending levels achieved by Reagan would be restored.

Despite Ronald Reagan's inability to achieve his fiscal goals, and despite George Bush's reversal of even the modest gains of the Reagan Evolution, there is one aspect of the 1981 economic recovery program that is now firmly in place and will be for some time to come. That is Reagan's original monetary policy, which was so badly violated during the first six and a half years of his presidency. In the summer of 1987, President Reagan appointed Alan Greenspan to replace Paul Volcker as chairman of the Federal Reserve. Greenspan then proceeded methodically to manage the money supply with astonishing fidelity to Reagan's original prescription, gradually reducing money growth down to almost zero.

The following table shows the annual rate of growth of M-2 since 1987:

1988	5.5%
1989	5.1%
1990	3.5%
1991	3.0%
1992	1.5%
1993	0.5%

The result of this policy is that the United States is truly on its way to breaking the back of inflation (the consumer price index has fallen from its perch above 6 percent three years ago to 2.8 percent currently). In addition, as the inflation premium has been squeezed out of interest rates, they have fallen to their lowest level in decades.

Of course, slowing money growth also caused the 1990 recession, an unavoidable way station on the road to a noninflationary environment. The recession was wrongly blamed on the Bush tax hike, and this error in turn gave conservatives false hope when President Clinton, following the trail blazed by Bush, raised taxes after winning the presidency on a promise to cut them. Many Republicans leaped to the doomed conclusion that Clinton would suffer the same fate that Bush suffered, namely, a recession and political defeat. They were wrong on both counts. Bush's unwise tax hike did not cause a recession, nor will Clinton's. The economy had started to slow in 1989 and actually fell into recession in the third quarter of 1990 (July-September). The tax bill was not signed until October. It had barely gone into effect when the economy started pulling out of the recession in the second quarter of 1991. Since then, despite the tax hike, the economy has experienced ten consecutive quarters of economic growth.

Conservatives need to understand this point, otherwise they will fail to appreciate the importance, both economic and political, of monetary policy. It is true that excessive taxes discourage investment and enterprise. They are an economic depressant. They reduce the efficiency of the economy. But they are not the cause of the business cycle, as such, which is a monetary phenomenon. High taxes lower the peaks and deepen the troughs of the business cycle; they are not its primary determinant.

A classic case in point was the 1932 tax increase. Conservatives properly criticize Herbert Hoover's mistake in raising taxes during a depression, but they need to remember that the tax increase came at the cyclical double bottom of the Great Depression, which was followed immediately by a cyclical recovery that lasted 50 months and produced annualized growth of 12 percent, the fastest since the Civil War.

Bill Clinton's $50 billion per year tax increase, though unwise and a breach of faith with the American people, is peanuts in a $5 trillion economy. It will surely make us a little worse off, but, like the Hoover and Bush tax bills, it will not stop the recovery in its tracks. If marginal tax rates approaching 40 percent on the mega-rich are incompatible with economic expansion, how was it that John F. Kennedy's boom in the sixties—so celebrated by contemporary conservatives—could occur, given that the top marginal rate never once fell below 70 percent ?

BILL CLINTON: POLICY WONK OR PROGRESSIVE SUPERSTAR

When President Clinton had trouble finding his sea legs in the early months of his presidency, many Republicans gleefully wrote off his chances for re-election. This was the shallowest kind of wishful thinking. President Kennedy's first few months in office were a catalogue of incompetence, from the Bay of Pigs to the Vienna Summit, and yet JFK subsequently attained some of the highest approval ratings ever recorded by a president. My own view of Clinton so far is that he is a risk taker, a fighter, and a realist who makes tactical retreats but never strategic ones. His narrow victories on NAFTA and the budget would seem to confirm that view.

But the most interesting aspect of Clinton's economic policy in his first year has nothing to do with the sound and fury of the policy debates but with the silence of the dogs that did not bark. Neither the president nor his top economic advisers have engaged in any Fed bashing, and indeed, the president sent Hillary Rodham Clinton to court Alan Greenspan at the very outset of the administration. From a narrowly partisan point of view, this should be a chilling warning to those Republicans who believe that Clinton, like Carter before him, will turn out to be an Inspector Clouseau in economic matters, a hapless, incompetent bungler.

On the contrary, Clinton seems to have grasped that he can avoid being "Carterized" by skyrocketing inflation and interest rates so long as Alan ("Whip Inflation Now") Greenspan stays the course he has been on for the past six years.[8] If this is, in fact, President Clinton's thinking, it is unlikely that there will be any Fed bashing so long as the economy continues to grow, as it has for the past 31 months and as it appears likely to do indefinitely.

In this connection, there was a remarkably optimistic assessment of this recovery's longevity in the *Wall Street Journal* for November 8, 1993, under the title, "Expansion May Prove Long Distance Runner." The author, Alfred Malabre Jr., is a most knowlegable student of the business cycle, and he points out that the current upswing already compares favorably with a majority of the economic recoveries of the past century and a half:

> The business expansion, for all the recent shakiness in the stock and bond markets, may well prove remarkably durable. After 31 months, it already has outlasted 17 of the 31 earlier business-cycle upswings that economists have traced since the middle of the last century. If the expansion endures only a few more months, its length will exceed the average for all its predecessors.
>
> This seems likely. The economy may, in fact, still be in the relatively early stages of an unusually long growth period.

The reason for this, as Malabre points out, is that the pace of the expansion is modest or indeed even sluggish by comparison with past expansions. This slow pace, in turn, is consistent with Greenspan's determination to let recovery unfold on a timetable set by the economy's natural restorative powers rather than to goose or to gun the economy with artificial monetary stimulus.

The prospect of good economic news coming out of the Clinton administration has provoked Robert J. Barro, professor of economics at Harvard, to make an extraordinary suggestion. He thinks that Alan Greenspan deserves the lion's share of the credit for the good news, and should therefore resign![9]

Professor Barro notes that the "misery index" (which candidate Reagan used with devastating effectiveness against President Carter in the 1980 debates) is improving under President Clinton. In fact, it is now down almost to where it was when Ronald Reagan left office.

> . . . the misery index score is not bad, and Mr. Clinton owes this result to a monetary policy that has kept down inflation and interest rates. Over the past several years, the maintenance of low inflation and the declining expectations of future inflation derive from the commitment of the Federal Reserve and its chairman, Alan Greenspan, to a policy of reasonable price stability. Moreover, Mr. Clinton has been very clever to support Mr. Greenspan and to avoid attacks on the Fed's independence and, hence, its credibility. (Mr. Clinton perhaps learned from the experience of Jimmy Carter, for whom a disastrous monetary policy was the main source of trouble in the domestic area.)

For Professor Barro, however, Greenspan's sterling performance in the service of his country has at last become problematic. The silver cloud has a dark lining.

> Although the nation benefits from monetary stability, this same stability—and the consequent good performance of the financial markets—makes it easier for the administration to enact an array of undesirable interventions into the economy. If the stock and bond markets were less bouyant, then the government would be more reluctant to raise taxes or minimum wage rates or to implement a remarkably expensive health care plan.
>
> Mr. Greenspan has to ask whether, as a good libertarian, he can remain as part of an administration team that is basically promoting socialism. The longer he stays in office, the more he resembles Col. Nicholson (played by Alec Guinness) in "The Bridge on the River Kwai," who forgot his underlying mission and built a marvelous bridge for his Japanese jailers. The colonel finally woke up and said "What have I done?" just before falling on the detonator and blowing up the bridge. It would be better if Mr. Greenspan left the government a little further in advance of the explosion.

Without expressing an opinion as to whether Chairman Greenspan should resign,[10] I believe that Barro is making an absolutely correct point here, namely, that Greenspan's brilliant conduct of monetary policy, in the teeth of excessive spending, regulation, and taxation, is the primary cause of whatever health the economy enjoys. He is also absolutely correct that a healthy economy widens the range of policy options open to visionary planners like Ira Magaziner and Hillary Rodham Clinton. It would be no small irony if the belated implementation of Ronald Reagan's monetary policy fulfilled a necessary condition for the implementation of Bill Clinton's social program.

Which brings us back to the 1890s. In that decade, the money question—the silver debate—which had been a dominant theme of American politics for a quarter of a century, was laid to rest, for a couple of decades at least. What came to the fore then was a far broader and deeper debate, an intellectual eruption, that produced the three great progressive tsunamis of the twentieth century, separated by briefer periods of conservative consolidation. The first wave was the opening two decades of the century, the era of Theodore Roosevelt and Woodrow Wilson, followed by a decade of Harding, Coolidge and Hoover; the second was the thirties and forties, the New Deal of Franklin Roosevelt and Harry Truman, followed by a decade of Dwight Eisenhower; the third was the sixties and seventies, beginning with John F. Kennedy and Lyndon Johnson, ending with Jimmy Carter, and followed by the decade of Ronald Reagan.

Have we now witnessed the arrival, right on schedule, of the fourth great wave created by the intellectual explosion of a century ago? Are we about to see yet another quantum leap forward toward the kind of social and economic equality that is the goal of the activist state? Are Hillary Rodham and Bill Clinton the Eleanor and Franklin of the 90s?

The answer to these questions, I fear, is "yes." In keeping with the original Progressive dream of putting expertise in the service of equality, today's liberals are on the threshhold of attempting a radical extension of the notion of entitlements, beginning with universal health care under the benevolent eye of federal planners. This new thrust by the bureaucratic/progressive state may occur under optimal conditions, because the 1990s may be the best decade of the twentieth century, in the sense that they may be free of the wars (WWI, WWII, Vietnam) and the economic troubles that severely restricted reformers in the past.   Imagine, for a moment, Lyndon Johnson operating within a healthy monetary framework and without the constraints imposed by the "guns versus butter" debates of the sixties, and you will get an idea of what is possible.

As we drift gently into a time of peace and prosperity, we may not sense or feel anything oppressive about the next web of regulations that are woven around us.   We may find ourselves, not in an Orwellian nightmare but a painless Tocquevillean trance.[11]   In Bill and Hillary Rodham Clinton we see the mating of political cunning with bureaucratic courage, a union that may give birth to a new age in which, as was foretold in the progressive books of old, the government of men will be replaced by the administration of things.

Endnotes

1.   Anyone who reads Theodore Dreiser's great "Trilogy of Desire" (*The Financier, The Titan, The Stoic*) will not fail to be struck by the parallels between the 1880s and the 1980s. Michael Milken and Ivan Boesky—ruthless, unprincipled apostles of greed, as seen through the eyes of their detractors—are instantly recognizable in the character of Frank Cowperwood.

2.   This was part of a "revenue neutral" deal whereby the upper marginal tax rate on individual incomes was reduced to 28 percent.

3.   In my (minority) view, there are no theoretical issues between monetarists and advocates of the gold standard, whether they be supply-siders or Austrians. The only genuine issue is the practical one of which approach is more effective in restraining the inflationists.   Both monetarists and gold standard advocates believe that money, in the long run, is a veil, and that real factors (e.g., natural resources, the skill of the labor force, etc.) determine economic growth. I believe that slow, steady growth of the money supply (monetarism) would result in a

steady gold price, just as it would result in steady consumer and commodity price indexes (even though the prices of individual consumer goods and commodities would change relative to each other). Likewise, targeting the price of gold would result in slow, steady growth of the money supply. The two approaches logically entail one another.

With respect to the practical issue, I do not agree that the United States experienced inflation in the seventies because we went off the gold standard (or what was left of it) in 1971. I think we went off the gold standard because we had inflation. However, that may be, the root cause of inflation is a political unwillingness to exercise the necessary self-restraint to curb excessive, inflation-causing money growth. It was that political failure that led to the final abandonment of gold and it was that same political failure that led to uncontrolled money creation.

4.   This analysis considers monetary policy in isolation from fiscal and regulatory policy, but of course a complete account of the factors contributing to peak economic efficiency could not ignore them.

5.   "Instead of evenly spreading the reduction in money growth over a six year period, the Federal Reserve delivered 75 percent of the reduction in the first year." Paul Craig Roberts, *The Supply-Side Revolution*, Cambridge: Harvard University Press, 1984, p. 116.

6.   This analysis by Scott A. Hodge and Robert Rector of the Heritage Foundation (Backgrounder #886) excludes the S&L bailout and net interest costs from domestic spending.

7.   In the Senate only six Republicans voted against the Americans With Disabilities and Clean Air acts. In the House only 17 voted against the former and 16 against the latter.

8.   Greenspan, of course, had been a member of President Ford's economic team, during a time when the government's effort to fine tune the economy made it a laughingstock. In the year Ford took over from Nixon after Watergate, inflation was running at 10 per cent. This led to the administration's slogan, WIN (Whip Inflation Now). The slogan was no sooner on everyone's lips than Ford sudenly realized that the economy was spiralling into deep recession. He dropped WIN like the political hot potato it was, and turned to old reliable, the money supply. Taking as his motto IN (Inflate Now!), Ford revved up the money supply (M-2), which shot upward at the astonishing rates of 12.6 percent in 1975 and 13.7 percent in 1976, rates which even Carter at his worst was never able to equal. The result was predictable. The economy rocketed out of recession, a hair too late for Ford, whose only consolation was that

his irresponsible monetary policy had sparked the inflation of the late seventies that wrecked Carter's presidency. Surely these events must have been on Greenspan's mind when he became chairman of the Federal Reserve. It's hard to forget a bad snakebite.

9.   Robert J. Barro, "The New Socialism," *Wall Street Journal*, October 25, 1993, p. A14.

10. a) Greenspan won't resign; b) even if he does, that doesn't guarantee that the other inflation hawks on the Fed will; and c) if President Clinton is afraid—as Barro suggests he might be—of being Carterized, then there is nothing to prevent him from appointing a Greenspan clone.

11. Trance: from Old French *transe*, from *transi*r, "to pass (from life to death)."

— 3 —

Hopes and Fears of a New Democrat

David K. Nichols

On November 15, 1993 Lane Kirkland of the A.F.L.-C.I.O. charged that President Clinton, in his campaign to win approval of NAFTA, had "clearly abdicated his role as leader of the Democratic party." Such criticism by a major labor leader might have been sufficient to write the obituary of any Democratic president from FDR to Carter. According to most sources, however, we are witnessing not the death but the rebirth of the Clinton Presidency. For the first time in his Presidency Clinton has demonstrated a willingness to stand firm against powerful opposition and bend Congress to his will.

Conventional wisdom suggests that while Clinton's actions may have created some tension between the White House and organized labor, the tension will be relieved when Clinton returns to those issues where he is in fundamental agreement with the labor movement. The success of Clinton on NAFTA will enhance the image of his presidency, create renewed respect for Clinton among members of Congress and propel

Clinton to victory on more traditional Democratic issues such as health care.

Organized labor, environmentalists, black leaders and other opponents of NAFTA are likely to become reconciled with Clinton, but Lane Kirkland's words are nonetheless instructive. Clinton claims to be a new Democrat, leading his country and his party to a bright future, but in order to be successful at that task he must come to grips with the forces that animate the old Democratic Party. The NAFTA vote is eloquent testimony to the difficulties involved in that task.

NAFTA was a Clinton victory but it was decidedly not a Democratic victory. Only 40 percent of House Democrats voted for NAFTA whereas an overwhelming majority of Republicans supported the president. This is not a great surprise. Although there are important Democrats who have supported free trade, as well as Republican isolationists such as Pat Buchanan, from the beginning NAFTA has been more closely associated with Republicans than Democrats.

No one expressed the reasons for this division better than Clinton: the supporters of NAFTA are the voices of hope, the opponents of NAFTA are the voices of fear. The opponents fear the future, they fear competition, and most of all they fear that any gains by others must come at their expense. For the opponents of NAFTA economics is about redistribution not production, about protecting one's piece of the pie, rather than making more and bigger pies.

The opponents of NAFTA should remind us of nothing so much as the populists of the late 19th century. This may seem a strange analogy. After all it was the populists who opposed high protective tariffs and supported free trade. But free trade was only a part of the populist agenda. The animating force of the populist agenda arose from a desire to protect the small farmer from the power of big business. People were being driven off their farms by changing economic circumstances. Big business was replacing agriculture as the dominant economic force in the country. The Populist attack on big business was based on the assumption that the growth of big business was responsible for the plight of the small farmer and that only by checking the power of big business could the small farmer be saved.

The populists were wrong then just as the opponents of NAFTA are wrong today. The plight of the small farmer was the product of increased productivity of all farmers. The number of farms was decreasing precisely because technology was increasing farm productivity. Agriculture was and is a major success story of the American economy, but a major part of that success is that the production of agricultural goods no longer requires massive amounts of labor. No one would suggest that we replace our tractors with horse drawn plows in order to recover the jobs that have been lost in the agricultural sector.

The story is the same today in manufacturing. The number of manufacturing jobs in this country has remained stagnant from the early 1970s to the present. But in that same period manufacturing output in the United States has doubled. This is not a sign of a lack of competitiveness, but of the opposite. We have become more competitive, but that means in part that we produce more goods with less labor. Organized labor wants to protect manufacturing jobs, but the protection of jobs would mean a rejection of competitiveness and increased productivity, a policy that would surely lead to fewer jobs of any kind over the long run. The only way to overcome the loss of jobs in the manufacturing sector is to find or create new markets for U.S. products and to shift the labor force into different types of jobs. Such changes entail risks, and risks are not popular with those who practice a politics of fear.

In the 1890s the Democratic Party was captured by the populists. In 1896 they nominated William Jennings Bryan and in so doing they identified themselves as the party of the past, the party that feared the future. They lost in 1896 and went on to nominate Bryan two more times, and to lose every presidential election until the Republican vote was split between Taft and Theodore Roosevelt in 1912. But Bill Clinton is no William Jennings Bryan. He won in 1992, although that victory was in part made possible by a substantial defection of Republican voters to Ross Perot. Clinton campaigned as a new Democrat who would accept the challenge of the future rather than repeat the promises of the past. And, Clinton's support for NAFTA is the mark of a new Democrat who refuses to be trapped by the fears and dogmas of the old Democrats.

But if the NAFTA vote provides evidence that Clinton is a new Democrat, it provides even more striking evidence that the Democratic Party is still dominated by the politics of fear. In spite of a massive lobbying effort, the promises of pork, and most important of all the fear that a loss for Clinton on NAFTA would cripple the first Democratic president since Carter, only 40 percent of the Democrats were willing to vote yes on NAFTA. If we were to take away the pork, presidential persuasion and fear of presidential meltdown, how many Democratic votes for NAFTA would have remained? Where is the evidence for a new Democratic Party?

More to the point, where beyond NAFTA is there evidence that Clinton himself is a new Democrat? Let us briefly review the major issues of Clinton's first year in office. In addition to his NAFTA success Clinton has issued executive orders reversing the Reagan-Bush policy on abortion counseling, developed a new policy on gays in the military, and passed a family leave bill and a national service bill. With the possible exception of national service, each of these policies reflects old liberal Democratic dogma. There is nothing in these policies to make Clinton a new Democrat.

Clinton has, however, been willing to moderate his initial liberal policy preferences. For example, he unambiguously expressed his desire to end the ban on gays in the military, but when it came time to implement the policy Clinton had to engage in considerable backtracking to avoid a revolt in Congress.

The national service bill presents a more complicated case. Although the bill may be anathema to libertarians on the left and right, over the years a number of Republicans and Democrats have supported the idea of a national service bill. Clinton's initial proposal, however, was for the creation of a massive new entitlement program aimed less at encouraging national service than at creating a new financing scheme for higher education. Once again Clinton's policy inclinations were traditionally liberal. But also once again, Clinton retreated from his initial proposals. Responding to Congressional pressure Clinton accepted a bill that was greatly reduced in terms of scope and funding. One might be pleased that Clinton has been willing to moderate his initial liberal proposals, but one should not misunderstand this moderation. Clinton did not change his mind about his policy goals, he was merely unwilling to stand firm and fight when faced with pressure from various interest groups. In this respect Clinton combined two of the worst traits of the old Democrats—a reflexive commitment to liberal polices and a hypersensitivity to interest group pressure from any direction.

The appointments process has also been plagued by presidential inconsistency. Clinton's commitment to group representation led to one disaster after another in his choice of an Attorney General. It was obvious that Clinton was focusing on gender first and other qualifications second, and the shortcomings of such an approach became equally obvious. His desire to appease various interest groups in the selection of a Supreme Court Justice almost distracted him from the politically successful nomination of Ruth Bader Ginsburg. Ginsburg was an obvious frontrunner for the position, but her willingness to suggest that there might be problems with the legal reasoning of *Roe* v. *Wade* moved her off of the short list. Ginsburg is no conservative, but her case showed that any break with liberal articles of faith could be damning. Only after the nomination process bogged down, and it appeared that Clinton might even be reduced to nominating a white male for the Court was Ginsburg rehabilitated.

On foreign policy Clinton has been rightly praised for his steadfast support for Boris Yeltsin, but in every other area of foreign policy Clinton has shown the contradictions involved in a Carter-like belief in an abstract notion of human rights and a liberal reluctance to make a sustained commitment of American forces. He blames Bush for not acting in Bosnia, but his own lack of resolve was so obvious he could not garner support from the Europeans who have a direct interest in the conflict. He unquestioningly accepted the U.N. Secretary-General's call to shift efforts from food distribution to nation building in Somalia, and when the difficulty of such a task became obvious he scrambled to find a way out that would cover the fact that he had made a commitment that he was not prepared to honor.

During the campaign he was indignant over Bush's callous treatment of Haitian refugees, but when in office he soon recognized that Bush's policy was the only practical one. Nonetheless he made the equally impractical promise that he would return Aristide to power, only to be surprised that virtually unarmed American military personnel would not be able to accomplish the task. His problems in foreign policy thus mirror his problems in domestic policy. A combination of a commitment to abstract liberal principles and a hypersensitivity to political pressure do not make for a sound policy and they do not make a new Democrat. They merely reflect the worst of the old Democratic party.

Nowhere does this fact become more obvious than on the two issues that will make or break Clinton's presidency in the long run—the economy and health care. Clinton's deficit reduction package is certainly less significant than he claims. Although Clinton says it will reduce the deficit, the reductions are based on an artificially high estimate of the future deficits. The fact is that according to Clinton's own estimates the deficit will remain at virtually the same level over the next five years.

Clinton's supporters claim that Clinton at least had the courage to take on special interests in the budget, but little about the budget supports that claim. Other than defense there are few cuts in major programs. The major deficit reduction comes from a $246 billion tax increase, an idea we didn't need new Democrats to develop. Moreover, the budget actually proposes spending $74.9 billion on new programs. The budget might have been worse. The economic stimulus package and the more extensive energy tax proposed by Clinton might have become law if Clinton had been a more effective legislative leader. But whatever small amount of moderation we find in the final budget, it can hardly be attributed to Clinton's vision as a new Democrat.

It is hard to see health care as the issue on which Clinton will establish his break with the policies of the past. From the symbolism of a national health care card to the substance of a massive new program that will bring at least 1/6th of the U.S. economy under the management of the federal government, Clinton's health care proposals harken to the entitlement philosophy that is at the core of the old Democratic party.

What most of Clinton's policies have in common is that they reflect the very values Clinton rejected in the debate over NAFTA. They represent an appeal to the fears and insecurities of the American people. Only massive government efforts can save you from the indifferent or sinister forces that control your lives. You must be protected from those forces, because you are powerless as an individual to deal with them. But such protection comes at a cost, a cost of greater dependency, of less freedom. Higher taxes mean that government will have more say and individuals will have less say over the way the money they earn will be spent. Managed health care means that in addition to dealing with doctors, hospitals and insurance companies, you would also have to take into account limits imposed by a government bureaucracy in making decisions about your health care.

People turn to government out of fear, and sometimes those fears are legitimate. Sometimes people need protection. But Clinton's policies are based on the belief that fear is the dominant force in American politics today. In this respect Bill Clinton and Ross Perot represent the same side in American politics. They believe that they can lead people to accept even welcome government protection if they can tap into their fears.

There is one important difference between Clinton and Perot. For Perot the deepest fears of the American people are fears of foreigners taking their jobs. He wants to protect us from people in other countries who do not share our aspirations or our values, from people whom he claims aspire only to having an outhouse. To his credit Clinton rejects such ignoble fears.

At the same time, Clinton is more than willing to play on other fears that are just as distasteful. He is willing to play the politics of race, gender, and class in order to build political support. When he suggests that New Yorkers who fail to vote for Dinkins are racists, when he attacks those with different views on civil rights or social welfare policy as racists, when he appeals to groups on the basis of their status as victims, when members of his administration describe religious leaders as prejudiced or dogmatic because they dare to hold values different from the Democratic party, when he speaks of the evil people who prospered in the eighties, Clinton is appealing to the same politics of fear he finds so repugnant in Ross Perot.

The Democratic party has increasingly become a Congressional party, a party that bases its claim to rule on its ability to provide government protection for the special interests created by the welfare state. The success of that party is based on its ability to convince the American people that security can only be found at the end of a government program. Individuals are told that they cannot possibly hope to deal with the world without the help and protection of government. They are told to find virtue in victimization and moral depravity lurking behind traditional success stories.

Clinton ran as the candidate from Hope, but to be a president who offers hope, he would have to reject many of the premises underlying the old Democratic party. He would have to reject the politics of fear and division. He would have to develop a domestic policy agenda that was based on the values he championed in NAFTA, a domestic policy that would celebrate the ability of individuals to compete, to become independent, and to cast off those fears that they are the victims of others.

All successful presidents have practiced the politics of hope, but for Clinton to do so he would have to risk the continued displeasure of Lane Kirkland and many other old Democrats. He would have to openly and honestly abdicate his claim as leader of the old Democratic party. But I suspect we will find that Clinton's fear of losing the support of old Democrats is greater than his hope for building a new majority coalition.

— 4 —

Understanding Clinton:
A Transatlantic View

John Zvesper

In Britain as in the United States, the keynote assessments of Clinton's first year is uncertainty. There is uncertainty, first of all, about what the Clinton administration intends to accomplish. There is uncertainty about what it has managed to accomplish. And there is uncertainty about what it should accomplish. Part of this unusual degree of uncertainty surrounding the Clinton administration is attributable to the fact that the post-Cold War world is proving to be a less predictable era than many had imagined or hoped a few years ago. Part of it must also be attributed to the hesitations and ambivalence of Clinton himself and of his associates: in domestic policy, are they new Democrats, or just updated New Deal Democrats? And do they or do they not have an intelligible foreign policy? Abroad, this latter question naturally figures more prominently in people's minds, and the low priority it has been given by Clinton thus increases the doubts about him. And of course, in Europe, perhaps especially here in Britain where they think they speak more or less the same language, there is the added complication that American politics is not always well understood. At the same time, those who wish Clinton well voice understanding, in the sense of excusing, so "understanding" Clinton often means mentioning all the barriers to his desires that are formed by the functioning and malfunctioning of the political system and by the fact that he has a very weak electoral mandate.

In spite of these various uncertainties, moderated by this sometimes pitiful attempt to be "understanding," there is emerging a rather clearly-defined set of criteria by which to assess the Clinton administration as it proceeds to define itself over the next few months. As far as domestic policy is concerned, these criteria seem to be shared to a remarkable extent by observers all along the ideological spectrum, although their judgments about the meaning of these criteria naturally differ. In a nutshell, left-wingers admire, while right-wingers denounce, Clinton's apparent strategy of basing his future popular support on extending the American people's dependence on the federal government. As far as American foreign policy goes, there is emerging a shared view that Clinton's America is—understandably—less interested in Europe and more interested in Asia and the Americas, and perhaps less interested in the outside world altogether; but there remains much uncertainty here as to what to make of this situation: should Europeans be grateful or anxious about the loosening of the apron strings?

Europeans see Clinton as a president who is very inexperienced in foreign and military affairs, and they have noticed the wavering and improvisation. Some commentators have taken cheap shots at this; for example, in June *The Times* suggested that Warren Christopher might have been the perfect Secretary of State had the ozone layer been America's greatest foreign policy challenge. But there is also a more serious concern with American foreign policy, and a genuine appreciation of the difficulty of choosing (if that luxury is allowed) between foreign policy minimalism and a newly-defined globalism, and—even if minimalism is chosen—the difficulty of defining America's national interest. There are perceptions, sometimes accompanied by fears, that American foreign policy has been subordinated to American economic policy; thus in November, after several weeks of public debate on NAFTA and preparation for the December GATT decision, the diplomatic correspondent of *Die Zeit* took comfort from the American opinion polls that showed an uneasy reaction to Clinton's unidealistic, mercantilist foreign policy style. Because the world needs a strong international order, he remarked, the world cannot afford for America to become another Japan.

On domestic policy, there has been more clearly defined action by Clinton, and probably not more but certainly more definite reaction. Early in the year, at least up to June (when David Gergen joined the White House), European reactions to the new administration were characterized by disappointment, and by fear either that Clinton was not up to the job or—more sympathetically—that the job of being president has become too impossible for anyone, however able, to do. This latter theme—that an understanding of the difficulties he faces excuses many of Clinton's failures—was about the only thing that sympathetic observers could say about Clinton in the first few months. As late as the beginning of August (just before the narrow Clinton victory on the budget vote), a correspondent for *The Guardian*, a center-left newspaper, could write in praise of Clinton only that his "consistent underachievement, in contrast to Bush's over-reaching, suggests a better understanding of the limitations of presidential power." Modern presidents, especially after the end of the Cold War, simply lack "the ability to control events." The idea that the end of the Cold War has brought greater demands from citizens on domestic policies—and therefore on politicians—is pretty well established in Europe (as well it might be, given Europeans' own experiences); thus European commentators are ready to understand Clinton's problems in that light as well. However, some Europeans also wonder why Americans seem to be so disenchanted with their system of government, because they feel that America has, after all, not done so badly. These days when I teach my students about the malfunctioning "new American political system"—legislators reduced to ombudspersons, isolated presidents, hyperactive courts and bureaucrats, inactive and cynical citizens—they now ask me how such a system has managed to preside over such worldly success. A healthy question, if only because it goes against the tendency for us political scientists to provide the politicians that we study with so many excuses for their behavior! Even *The Guardian*'s correspondent admitted that in his first six months in office Clinton had displayed "a natural's talent for truly spectacular ineffectiveness which his tendency to fudge, dodge and compromise only exacerbates." And in fact, contrary to the "understanding" view, some of the most spectacular failures of the early days of the Clinton administration can be put down not to the weakness of the presidency but to its strength. Perhaps unfortunately for Clinton, certain actions touching issues like federal funding of abortions, homosexuals in the military, and ponderous attention to "egg" (ethnicity, gender, geography) in appointments, were within his executive powers; his actions on these matters caused controversies within his own party, raised the country's doubts about his new Democrat credentials, and, as he admitted, weakened his promised "laser-beam" focus on the economy. We may well be living through "an era of presidential impotence," but in politics presidents' actions and inactions still matter more than anyone else's, and they can and no doubt will be held responsible for the way they use their powers.

The improvement in the Clinton record of achievement and public approval after the first few miserable months proves this point, for it owes as much to Clinton's relaunching of his administration as it does to good luck. His appointment of David Gergen in June was seen here as a somewhat puzzling turning point, with obvious dividends in the reduction of gaffes made much of by the press, but also with uncertain implications about the substance, as opposed to the image, of Clinton's presidency. For example, the attack on Baghdad, in rather tardy retaliation for the Iraqi plot against George Bush, was seen as a popularity and image-improving move more than a defining step in the emergence of a Clinton foreign policy. The uncertainty about the direction of the administration remains, and the suspicion is often voiced that for all the talk of a shift back to "centrist" positions, Clinton remains wedded, in more ways than one, to a not-very-new liberal Democratic program. Attitudes to this vary, but the perception is widely shared.

On the domestic front, the health care program is seen as the defining policy. An article in the *Spectator* at the beginning of November, "The Bribing of America," asserted that the Clintons' emphasis on security threatens American individualism and self-reliance. A fortnight later, the *Times Literary Supplement* carried the same message, although from a more sympathetic (left-wing academic) source: "Although the health care plan is being presented as modern, regulated capitalism, it is actually a Robin Hood scheme in the best social democratic tradition." Celebrating what the *Spectator* writer was deploring, this *TLS* writer interpreted Clinton's policies as a sign that the European left need not "mutate" in the direction of Thatcher and Reagan in order to survive: if Americans can be increasingly left-wing, then surely the Europeans can, too. If these identical judgments of the meaning of Clinton's presidency from the right and the left are accurate, then the immediate future of the republic would seem to depend on whether that crucial part of the electorate, the Reagan Democrats, can be wooed back to regular loyalty to the Democratic party by appeals to entitlements and to fears of insecurity. If they can, then Alexis de Tocqueville's worry about the attractiveness of the "soft despotism" of the parental state will again turn out to be one of the most useful ways of thinking about the tendencies of the modern democratic world.

But other developments lend support to a less gloomy conclusion, and suggest that Clinton (the husband if not the wife) is poised to move off in a more genuinely novel Democratic direction, which takes him closer to bipartisan cooperation than to New Deal-style state partisanship. Interrupting the flow of the health care debate has been the NAFTA debate. Observers in Europe noticed that Clinton's victory drew more support from Republican than from Democratic legislators; they were less likely to remark that in this debate the president and his vice-president waved the banners not of economic insecurity and anxiety but of opportunity and optimism. The ability of Clinton to prove himself and his party truly renewed may depend on his translating this kind of appeal to other issues, and on his carrying more of his own party with him;

Reagan Democrats might be appealed to in these terms, even though trade union allegiances among them pulled them in the opposite direction on the NAFTA issue. One issue on which he might do this is the "other" security issue: violent crime. This became more apparent in some of the November 1993 elections. As so often in the past, the New Jersey and Virginia gubernatorial races have been taken as important barometers. The situation in 1993 can be compared to that in 1985, when a Republican governor was re-elected in New Jersey by continuing to appeal to conservative Democratic voters, and a Democrat was elected in Virginia by (as Frank Fahrenkopf, then chairman of the Republican National Committee, complained at the time) "out-Republicanizing us." But in 1993 the crucial emerging issue seems to be not the economy but violent crime. In New Jersey, the Democratic incumbent, Jim Florio, lost the election, in part because he helped raise taxes. (This race was also reported here by hopeful social democrats with an eye on the prospects for tax and spend programs in Europe, since it looked like Florio was about to win.) But while losing the race, Florio gained votes by sounding tough on crime. And in Virginia, George Allen won partly on that same issue. The first impact of the emergence of crime (and drugs) as top concerns of the electorate has been the reduction of Clinton's approval ratings (and an increase in the percentage—to over 50 percent—of those who think Mrs. Clinton has too much influence over her husband). Yet he has shown (from the early days of his presidential candidacy down to his mid-November speech at Memphis) that he too is capable at least of talking tough on this issue. He is usually careful to include in his proposed solutions an emphasis on the importance of jobs; as he said at Memphis, in fine Aristotelian fashion, "Work organizes life." This raises again the question whether new

Democrat or New Deal Democrat policies on job creation are to be pursued, and whether self-reliance or reliance on the state is to be encouraged.

One of the reasons for the continuing uncertainties about such questions is that Clinton shares with other "reinventing government" fans the idea that ideas matter less than what works. Michael Dukakis can be seen as the Democrats' first new Democrat presidential nominee, when he tried to argue that the election of 1988 was about competence rather than ideology. Clinton, whose 1992 electoral strategy built on the Dukakis base, has to ponder the weakness of that base in a two-way race. Why is the attempt to avoid ideology so attractive to politicians today? Recall that George Bush started down that road in the 1988 election, too (turning back only when his claims based on his "resumé" or "experience" proved to be a losing strategy) and that he, like Clinton in many of the successful ventures of his second half-year, often relied on a bipartisan legislative strategy. Leading politicians of both of the major parties have been shying away from ideological and partisan warfare. They do this in response to that part of the public that is disenchanted with liberal-conservative divisions, and neutral towards partisan labels. They know very well that far more Americans identify themselves as moderates than as either conservatives or liberals (the meaning of "moderate" changes, but it remains opposed to ideological extremes), and that electoral identification with the major party labels, where it survives at all, is often a variable dependent on individual candidates' appeals rather than an independent variable determining candidates' electoral fortunes.

But however sensitive it is to public sentiment, there are dangers lurking in this end-of-ideology, end-of-party school of thinking. Clinton understands the popular basis of this school's appeal, but does he understand the dangers? The key difficulty with the anti-ideological approach to government is that although "reinventing government" presents itself as a *results*-oriented approach, impatient with ineffective methods, it is more accurately characterized as a *means*-oriented approach, which either takes political ends for granted (the old New Deal ends adjusted for the late twentieth century, say) or treats ends as unnecessary considerations in politics: the "boundless sea" view of the element of the ship of state. David Osborne and Ted Gaebler, the authors of the recently-published book *Reinventing Government*, state very clearly in the preface their conviction that "the central failure of government today is one of *means*, not *ends*." The paperback edition of this book carries on its front cover some uncharacteristically concise advice from Bill Clinton: "Should be read by every elected official in America. This book gives us the blueprint." Notice that the recommendation is not that ordinary citizens or even aspiring politicians should read the book, but that already-elected officials should read it: in other words, first get yourself elected, however you can and must, and then apply the book's advice. The book's advice—much of it very wise—is that the *process* of government can be greatly improved by breaking away from the assumption that government bureaucracies can provide the low-cost, high-choice kind of service that citizens are (or should be) now demanding in public programs such as education, housing, transportation and health care. Osborne and Gaebler call for "entrepreneurial government" which does more with less, imitating the successful managerial styles preached by management gurus such as Peter Drucker, Tom Peters and Robert Waterman. They chart the developments of these new managerial techniques by officials especially at the state and local level who have been encouraged to think about more effective and productive ways of doing their jobs, freed from unnecessary bureaucratic rules. Their basic argument is that Americans—like other modern countries—are finding that they do not need less government (the conservative line) or more government (the liberal line) but better government. More precisely, they say there is a need for better "governance"; the emphasis, always, is on the process and not the ends: "Governance is the process by which we collectively solve our problems and meet our society's needs."

This is evidently a seductive doctrine. (It has its champions in Britain, too, where there is currently a growth industry in management education.) Doubtless it has much to teach American citizens and politicians. But how can it be translated into politics, in any form but the populistic simplifications of a Ross Perot? The problems confronting the American polity are surely matters of *defining* the "problems" and "needs" of the country, and of deciding which of those problems and needs are properly addressed by (various levels of) government. One can agree that most government organizations can be made more effective—although the conservatism that is in truth the source of the government reinventers' skepticism about bureaucracy would point out that there is also the danger of overly-imaginative "entrepreneurial" officials!—and still disagree intelligibly and deeply about those fundamental political matters. If these substantive matters are relegated to mere electoral politics and image making, "reinventing government" promises not to cure but rather to deepen the alienation of citizens from their governments. To the government reinventers, "empowerment" of citizens means mainly treating them as "customers" with choices about government services that they receive, instead of as "clients" with little say.

But neither clients nor customers are liberal democratic citizens, and the better-serviced customers of reinvented government might just be even more contented subjects of a soft despotism.

Clinton's attraction to reinventing government is part of his great sympathy with and his understanding of the American people. Judged by the admittedly high standards of a Churchill, a De Gaulle, or even a Thatcher, he appears to be rather too close to popular sentiments to be able to step back and to help redefine them. A politician's being out of touch to some extent with the people can make him all the better at helping them to renew their identity.

— 5 —

The Politics of Meaning: Demeaning of Politics

Fred Baumann

At first sight, the chatter about Michael Lerner, the first lady's house philosopher, and his sloganeering "politics of meaning" has almost nothing to do with what has actually happened in the past year. Quite likely Nancy Reagan's astrologer had as much impact, i.e., almost none, on the eighties as Mrs. Clinton's Yoda will have had on the events of the early nineties.

Two things stand out in the last year's political doings: first, a fairly bumbling adjustment to being in power, accentuated by intellectual arrogance and naivete (e.g., the fiascoes of Bosnia and Somalia and the domestic disasters of the travel bureau and the Guinier nomination), and distorted by a touching desire to be universally liked; second, an administration that, whatever its radical tendencies, seems to be settling into an unprincipled centrist course that on occasion reminds me of nothing so much as its immediate predecessor. (It may be of course, that the image of bumbling, Bushy centrism is largely a mask and that the administration deserves credit for cunning long range leftism. For instance, the corporatist deal with Detroit could be read, *a la* Schumpeter, as getting the candidates for hanging to clamor for the rope. And perhaps it is not just conspiracy addicts who could suspect that the evidently underfinanced health care plan is designed to fail so that a public that has learned to expect universal care will arrive at "single payer" as the only alternative.) Still, I had certainly expected, going in, that the ideological Left of the party would do better than it has on its pet issues; I was surprised that Clinton withdrew Guinier's name and it seems that Ruth Bader Ginsburg is no Lawrence Tribe.

Overall, while it has been a liberal administration, Clinton's hasn't been a *very* liberal one. On the budget, caught in the vise grip of years of deficit spending, voted by Democratic Congresses, permitted by Republican presidents, Clinton has, it seems to me, done very little good but perhaps done harm mostly only by doing merely symbolic good. (Here it is worth referring to Irving Kristol's 1980 prophecy that even the failure of supply side economics would leave the Democrats in the mess they usually make for Republicans.) On health care, the difference between Clinton and the Republicans, while important and while characteristic of overall outlooks, seems in many ways technical and compromisable. And the decision to undertake the task in the first place, the greatest obvious difference between Clinton and Bush, is less attributable in my view to the leftist desire to tinker with absolutely everything than to Bush's smug belief that it was sufficient to have a domestic policy of frustrating whatever the Congress wanted. (To paraphrase Patrick Henry, if this was federalism, Bush sure didn't make the most of it.) In short, medicine has advanced so much in the last half century that our life chances really do depend greatly on the amount and kind of medical care we get and as a result, as Congressional Republicans now also admit, in a democratic society devoted to risk reduction, access to it can't be left to catch as catch can. Bush thus blew an opportunity and Clinton, tutored by James Carville, deserves neither great praise nor blame for noticing it.

On NAFTA, Clinton deserves credit for supporting it but seems to have left it till it is likely too late. Here is an issue which does not divide neatly right and left anyway; it is largely an elite vs. populist issue in which the populist side is thumpingly wrong. It was issues like this that led the Founders to arrange to have the Senate indirectly elected and the states to establish property qualifications for the vote. That is, it is an issue where immediate pain for some is traded for immediate, medium and long term gain for all. In politics, interests can hardly help screaming when hurt, (though the shortsightedness of the unions on this one doesn't do much to clear them from the charge of reaction) nor is the greater invulnerability of the monetarily unchallenged much to their moral credit. The fact remains that this kind of issue is a test of a nation's political health. The elites have to be confident enough to stand the barracking they will get from the Naders, Kirklands, Buchanans and Perots. Clinton's job here is to stand up against public opinion; indeed, here is where some of his New Class arrogance would (and Al Gore's has) come in handy. As I write, the vote hangs in the balance, and while Clinton has given it the old Yale try, it remains that he has not followed William Kristol's intelligent advice of giving an Oval office speech to the nation, putting all his prestige on the line and making of NAFTA first and foremost a national security issue.

And on foreign policy, Clinton's course has been determinedly centrist. His support of Yeltsin took some guts, given an elite media that is full of a strange spite against democratic Russia. (Not so strange perhaps; it can partly be explained by the lazy habit of applying ACLU standards to every regime that is friendly to us, partly too by a Gorby-crush they haven't gotten over yet and of course partly too—cf. Stephen Cohen's rebarbative presence on CBS and PBS—by the shame at having their rejection of the very possibility of democracy in Russia—which in turn functioned as backhanded apologias for the communist USSR—repeatedly shown up.)

On Somalia, muddled thinking and neglect made an overt botch out of what was probably an implicit botch when Bush undertook it. After all, what was supposed to happen when we had fed the starving and pulled out again? Either more civil war and more starvation or feeble, UN-based efforts at nation building. On Bosnia, as far as William Safire, whom I trust, can tell, Clinton's humane instincts came up against either Christopher's incompetence, his timidity, or his cold-blooded State Department professionalism, and lost. The policies that emerged in both places, while disasters, are certainly recognizably centrist disasters. On Haiti, ditto, though as I rewrite, it is (ever more faintly) possible that Clinton may even come off looking good, if the renewed embargo actually causes the military rulers to cave and allow the elected ruler, with all his rumored faults, to take over.

In the Middle East Clinton has had the good sense not to push the Israelis too hard when they were pushing themselves, to make their life a little easier at the time of the effort to exile the Hamas leaders, and to give extremely necessary moral support to Israel as it undertakes its momentous gamble. Of course Warren Christopher failed to get the Arab boycott of Israel lifted, even when no excuse for it exists any longer, but this does not suggest that he was not using his persuasive powers, such as they are, to the very maximum. Again, a centrist policy, and this time even a generally sensible one.

The "politics of meaning" then would seem to be a stylistic excrescence, about the same thing for Clinton as Bush's "new world order," his desperate grasp for something in the "vision thing" line. We actually have before us a politics of re-election, tempered somewhat by a desire to do a liberal's view of good whenever it's electorally safe. And so, safely ensconced in Yes Minister land, we can see the importance of having court poets or philosophers to give the illusion, so helpful to getting reelected, that one is not just interested in getting reelected but absorbed by the "politics of meaning." The meaning of the politics of meaning would thus be its meaninglessness.

If we look at the Clinton administration, as we have, from the viewpoint of Washington, of adherents and enemies, this line of argument makes sense. But if we look at it from outside, from the point of view of what is going on in the country the administration largely only pretends to govern, the politics of meaning has a real, and genuinely foolish, meaning.

The politics of meaning, in Hillary Rodham Clinton's version, as she explained it to Michael Kelly in the Sunday *New York Times* of May 23, 1993, is pretty thin and familiar stuff. She knows what she wants all right, e.g., Western society to be made anew, America rescued from a sleeping sickness of the soul, new meaning for our individual lives and our collective life, a community for each of us where we belong no matter who we are. And, like all good democrats since the hypocrite Meletus, she knows "who will lead us out of this spiritual vacuum," namely, of course, "all of us." However, when encouraged to descend from the purely to the merely partly gaseous, she has problems. "I don't know, I don't know," she confesses, "I don't have any coherent explanation." Still, like the A student who knows it's only a matter of turning her great and efficient brain squarely on the problem, she promises that "I hope one day to be able to stop long enough actually to try to write down what I do mean . . . because I have floated around the edges of this and talked about it for many, many years with a lot of people. . . ." Still, when forced to the wall, she admits (in oddly Bushian idiom) that the very core of what she believes is "this concept of individual worth." She has discovered that if you "break down the Golden Rule" and the command to love your neighbor as yourself, "there is an underlying assumption that you will value yourself." (Whew!) And pressed for specific examples we get three tips to Lady Bountiful: say to yourself, 1) "you know, I'm not going to tell that racist, sexist joke. I don't want to objectify another human being;" 2) "you know, I'm going to start thanking the woman who cleans the restroom in the building that I work in. . . . I want to start seeing her as a human being;" and 3) "how much are we paying this woman?"

Of course, we have not advanced one step beyond the nonsense of the Port Huron Statement, that terminal document of rentier capitalism. (Remember how it begins? "We are people of this generation, bred in at least modest comfort, housed now in universities, looking uncomfortably to the world we inherit.") Mrs. Clinton's tone is, like its predecessors, Port Huron and Carter's notorious "malaise" speech, vaguely uneasy and the substance is, even more than its predecessors, simply vague. The class comedy comes in with the question of who is the butt of some of the examples. Does the first lady mean that she has to take conscious thought before remembering that the cleaning woman is human? Or is she ever so politely pretending that she is referring to herself (after all, would *she* ever dream of telling a racist, sexist joke or objectifying another human being—not counting cookie bakers who stand by their men), while she is actually referring, in contemptuous and objectifying terms, to *other* bourgeois types to whom she believes herself superior? The breathtaking assumption that this drivel is thought, and that all she needs is time to write it all out in order to provide us with a rule of life, is both comical and troubling when we reflect that she is what passes for an educated person today. But for all that, this does represent the essential feelings of those New Leftists who decided to live cautiously enough to be where they are now, our rulers. As such, it is worth attention.

But not much. Still, one thing does stand out in most versions of the Gospel of the Sixties, including the first lady's. From Port Huron on, the New Left essentially accepted the description of American politics and institutions which was current among the sophisticated social scientists of the 1950s, itself an inheritance from the pragmatists and Progressives of an earlier time. What was announced as a refreshing break with the old constitutional piety by the likes of Woodrow Wilson, became the self-congratulatory hard-headedness of a Robert Dahl and was then turned into the lament of Tom Hayden and now Lerner-Clinton. Of course, what Dahl celebrated as pluralist, Hayden's master C. Wright Mills denounced as elitist. But the disagreement was founded on a considerable descriptive agreement. Because, the New Left saw the hard, skeletal structure of American politics as "value-free," and essentially instrumental, for use solely in interest conflict, (and thus wholly usable by the evil elites) it was compelled to find "meaning" only in the soft, amorphous, mollusk-like moistness in the interstices of the body politic. Hillary Rodham Clinton's incoherence faithfully follows Port Huron and for the same reason. Rational thought about the moral character of a nation by means of a consideration of its laws and institutions, had been forbidden (in fact forgotten) by the wise but evil forefathers like David B. Truman. All that was left, in both senses of the word, was a kind of colloidal piety, concocted, like a Jello recipe, of several vaguely related flavors, including a secularized Christian piety, vulgar Rousseauianism, vulgar Marxism, and contemporary feminism.

But whatever flavor dominates this confection, it can never be of much use, because from the outset it is designed as an attitude (above all an attitude of the morally self-conscious rich). It asks the well-off to recognize the humanity of cleaning women. It never asks the cleaning woman anything at all (and as such guarantees that it will never actually recognize her humanity, which of course includes her responsibility). It is invariably self-reflexive and narcissistic. Underneath it one can always hear the anxious hum of "how'm I doing?" It touches upon institutions without ever thinking about them, their inner nature, their implications. Thus, sufficient maundering about one's need to recognize the humanity of cleaning women leads the first lady to comparable worth, the policy as an expression of piety.

In this, the politics of meaning begins to reveal the fundamental failure of the generation of New Leftists who decided to work "within the system." Where there should be an intellectually consistent continuity between ends and means, from the highest theoretical and moral considerations to the most practical questions of instrumentality, with this generation there is a gaping discontinuity. On the one hand, the wooliest and most abstract pieties, on the other, the pettiest and narrowest kind of interest politics, and nothing much in between. Hence a plethora of quasi-Christian quasi-Machiavellis.

What makes the emptiness of the politics of meaning sad and frightening rather than merely comical or pathetic, is that the unease about our country that Hillary Rodham Clinton feels today seems to me far more justified than that of her model, Tom Hayden, thirty years earlier. The Clinton administration has not begun to face the real problems we face any more than did the Bush administration. Put simply, we are becoming increasingly barbarous. The request by the mayor of Washington D.C. for the militarization of the nation's capital isn't so much a straw in the wind as an RV in a tornado. So too are all those odd news stories about murders over a pair of socks, or chewing gum or (this morning on Columbus TV) a "dispute about coffee," (eh?) In these lurid stories we can trace the rebirth, in large parts of the nation, of an honor culture, a culture of hot-tempered, short-sighted, profoundly stultified and ignorant warriors. Indeed, I expect that a graph that would show the growth of preached standards of tolerance and sensitivity as well as the growth of mutual hatred and touchiness, might actually need only one line for the job. Indeed, the increasing ignorance, vulgarity, murderousness and above all touchiness of the population, and especially the young, are all fairly reliable and traditional indications that down the road a couple of decades even our solidest traditions of ordered liberty and self-government may be in big trouble. The Perot phenomenon is warning enough that a people that governs itself has to have some capacity to govern its fears and passions, for which education and moderation are needed. Frightened, superstitious and perpetually angry people make ideal Fascists but lousy Americans.

The first lady and her mentors are right that there is indeed a need for moral change and education in this country. But a strategy of moralism and pious ejaculations is, as they like to say, part of the problem, not part of the solution.

For there is an alternative to the diluted, namby-pamby religiosity of the politics of meaning, one which largely comes out of and not against our laws and institutions. Put tersely, it would be renewed thought about the implications and responsibilities of citizenship. Thus, a standard of citizen responsibility might reveal the indignity and folly of the current mania for group rights which seems to have brought us not only back to the days of race-based education but to those halcyon days of race-based (in)justice as well. Forgetfulness of the implications of citizenship lies behind affirmative action, which, by making group allegiances more important than citizenship, is the fundamental legal and political cause of that current domestic Balkanization so vividly illustrated once more by the Balkans themselves. Emphasis on citizenship might begin to rescue us from the corruption of taxation by amusement in the form of lotteries or from the libertarian excesses that deform every issue from abortion to gun control. There is, of course, some serious talk along these lines, to be found even among members of the Clinton administration, e.g., William Galston. Still, overall their voices are scarcely heard, drowned out by the drone of the dogmatic Old Left and the cant of the aged and saccharin New. And as long as the class and generation that rules America has only got the daily politics of barter and blame to work with, and the wet noodle of the politics of meaning to wave about in a feckless bid to avert vampires, the real and serious troubles of this country will continue to get more real and more serious.

— 6 —

In Defense of Red Tape

Larry P. Arnn

For three reasons, many conservatives welcomed the advent of Bill Clinton. To begin with, they greeted the new administration as a kind of national emetic. Appalled by the Bush jaundice, they recalled how the Carter years had purged us of bad humors. The Reagan tax plan was prepared in those years, in a Democratic Congress. The Reagan defense policy was foreshadowed in the Harold Brown Pentagon. Carter proved to be a wonderful set up man. Under him, liberals got distemper, and conservatives got well. That is his legacy.

Then too conservatives looked forward to what President Bill would *say*. Maybe he would, like President Jimmy, wring his hands in public as he discovered that his kind of government does not work. Or maybe he would actually go around talking conservative, about how government is too big, taxes too high, and only the military can do anything right. He did talk something like that in the campaign, which helped to prove that conservatives had "won the war of ideas" and "changed the debate forever."

Finally, conservatives were not too sad to see Clinton come *in* because they so looked forward to his going *out*, promptly and by acclamation. After that conservatives would have a real majority, and they would have the chance to use it without the distractions of the Cold War.

This optimism is so far partially vindicated. In a wave of elections at the local, state, and federal levels, Republicans have been sweeping into office. A number of Republican governors, mayors, lieutenant governors, U.S. and state senators, assemblymen and local representatives have lately won seats. In several states both houses and the governorship belong to the GOP, and most everywhere candidates distance themselves from the president or lose. Vouchers are coming to Jersey City. Gay rights are on the run. A property rights movement is growing at the grass roots, especially in the South and Northwest. People of color in big cities have voted for white Republicans. We may be on track for a big win

Before we consign the Clintons to the death that Carter died, we should however note some important differences between them. Both were southern governors, given no chance to win the presidency in the early going, and elected on anti-Washington themes. Only Clinton seems to understand what this means

Clinton is formidable politically for many reasons. They begin with his appreciation of the first fact of public opinion today, its disaffection with government. Each of his major domestic initiatives begins with an assurance that this is not business as usual. His economic plan recites the White House jobs he has cut, the executive dining rooms he has closed, and the limousines he has cancelled. He describes Washington as a city of "intrigue and calculation." His faith in God, which he avows often, serves for him and for "each of us—President,

Vice President, Senator, Congressman, General, Justice—as a source of humility. To remember that, as Bishop Sheen said, we are all sinners."[1] We are all sinners, but in Clinton's rhetoric the politicians are the sinners who get called by name.

Clinton is striving to remain apart from the system while commanding it. In this he reveals a deeper political understanding not only more than that of Jimmy Carter, but also George Bush's, who looked and acted what he was, a member of the establishment: A brave soldier, a good husband and father, a dutiful citizen, Bush managed to conceal these qualities behind a remoteness that seemed at one time cold, the next insensible, the third weak or stupid. He did not know, as Lincoln knew, the importance of the common touch. George Washington was revered almost as a monarch, but he assumed the simple title Mr. President. Even Churchill, the grandson of a Duke and offered the same title for himself, knew that only a commoner could rule a democratic people. This knowledge is essential to representative politics, and never more so than now, when the government itself is mistrusted deeply by those who have the right if not the means to control it.

The depth of the Clintons' appreciation of this point is apparent nowhere more than in Al Gore's exercise in reinventing government. Although the document, entitled the *National Performance Review* (hereafter *NPR*), was prepared by Gore, it was announced by the president himself and received by him with full ceremony. Several writers have greeted the *NPR* as an empty promise. More likely it marks a path that the Clinton administration will faithfully tread.

The *NPR* identifies itself with the most powerful movement in American business today. Led by Michael Hammer and James Champy, authors of *Reengineering the Corporation*, a generation of scholars, consultants, and managers are guiding industry in a relentless transformation. This transformation is made both necessary and possible by the combined influence of technology—above all computers—and competition. It seeks to locate and destroy every activity in the business that does not contribute tangibly to serving customers. In this process, no activity is seen as neutral: whatever does not serve the mission is the enemy. Everywhere businesses are adopting flatter structures, reducing their logistical tail—and eliminating jobs. This process is both urgent and painful. Even—or especially—companies that are doing well operate in constant apprehension for their survival.

The *NPR* adopts this tone for its own and applies it to that most wasteful, privileged, and protected of sectors—the federal government and its official legions. The *NPR* regales the reader with stories of agencies forbidden and commanded to do the same thing at the same time, of money scattered to the four winds, of bureaucrats moving at the pace of semi-molten lead. Spiced with quotations from General Patton and Werner von Braun, Thomas Jefferson and Abraham Lincoln, Tom Peters and Peter Drucker, *NPR* actually makes fair reading. It has some fun at the expense of the system, and then with earnest and upbeat tones it promises to fix it.

Several grudging writers have anointed this report as the one good thing (or, with NAFTA, one of the two good things) the Clintons have done in their first year. They contrast it with the tax increase and the health care plan, and they find contradiction. They claim either that the *NPR* is window dressing or that the Clintons are confused or schizophrenic. Neither is true.

In fact, the *NPR* is cut from the same cloth as the Health Security Plan. Like that plan, the *NPR* calls for changes that will expand the reach of the government and farther remove it from public control. Like that plan, it will treat the disease by introducing more of the virus that brought it on.

But how can it be bad? The *NPR* promises to cut civilian, non-postal staff by 12 percent, which it claims would bring it under two million for the first time since 1967. It promises to streamline procedures and to increase local control. It promises to save $108 billion over five years (about 1.5 percent of federal expenditures per year). Meanwhile, everybody will be happier: taxpayers, because they save; taxgetters, because they get treated like "customers"; and government workers, because they become part of a lean, mean system where everyone works really hard and gets to make plenty of decisions—for the public good, of course.

One can hardly help being charmed by this. Some parts of it sound very like the great speech that Ronald Reagan gave in 1964 that turned him into a politician and a presidential contender at the same time. But it soon parts company with the Reagan line, although it never troubles itself to admit the fact. The problem with *NPR* begins with its method and ends with its scope. Here is how Al Gore describes the method in his "Preface":

> We organized a team of experienced federal employees from all corners of the government—a marked change from past efforts, which relied on outsiders. We turned to the people who know government best—who know what works, what doesn't, and how things ought to be changed.

NPR is then a document prepared by "insiders." This time the system will be fixed by those who work in it. The standards of business are everywhere appealed to in this document. Leading business men are quoted in it frequently. But its foundation is laid by the people who staff the existing system. The result of this method is predictable. *NPR* is a manual for liberating the bureaucracy:

> Federal managers read the same books and attend the same conferences as private sector managers. They know what good management looks like. They just can't put it into practice—because they face constraints few managers in the private sector could imagine.

The "constraints" that federal managers face are graphically detailed in the report. Forestry workers have separate budgets for each activity they undertake: one for burning brush, another for mending fences, a third for building fences. Their budgets are "divided into 557 management codes and 1,769 accounting lines," and they cannot make the simplest transfers from one line to the other. Navy auto repair centers must get parts from a central supply center, and delays of weeks are common. Vehicles are therefore out of service for long periods, which means that the Navy must buy 10 percent more vehicles than it actually needs. *NPR* unfolds a long and sorry tale of false economy, contradictory rules, and thwarted effort.

The solution to this problem is generally, in *NPR*, to set the civil servants free from the constraints that hamper them. For example the inspectors general, created to prevent abuse in the bureaucracy, will now focus upon a new task. In addition to assuring that rules are followed, they will now consult with the bureaucracies they monitor to help them make their work more effective. Unless new staff are added, this job will detract from the old one, which was given to the inspectors because of a certain problem.

We can see the nature of this problem by considering an example in the *NPR* itself related by Vice President Gore. Federal marshals are allowed to seize the homes of drug dealers they apprehend and "use the money to finance the war on drugs." How they maintain the houses, while they are up for sale, is subject to the prevailing rules of procurement. If they want to get the lawns cut, for example, they cannot hire neighborhood kids to do it. Instead they must get bids from professional gardening services, which cost more. The bid process itself is expensive. Lots of money could be saved if this were not necessary. The *NPR* states that rules should be changed to permit the marshals to hire whom they please. Doubtless this is true.

On the other hand, consider the implications of such a change. Imagine one day that we have loosened the rules for procurement in these circumstances. We may well read about a ring of U.S. marshals who are using their authority to their own advantage. Many millions in real property are seized each year in major cities from drug raids. While these properties are in transition, they must be tended. Their roofs and plumbing, their carpeting and gardens all must be maintained, repaired, or upgraded. They must be sold. A fair price must be estimated, and someone must be paid for making the estimate, as another must be paid for making the sale. Of course a buyer must be found, and he will have an interest in getting the lowest price. Might he be willing to pay a little money to a government employee in order to get a better price? Might a gardener or a plumber be ready to pay something back to the civil servant in order to get the business? The interest of the employee and the interest of the vendor or buyer could easily come together in these circumstances.

This is the problem with bureaucracy. This is why those complicated rules have been written. They are designed to have one employee looking over the shoulder of the other, one process cancelling out or checking against the next. In government, people are dealing all the time with money and property that is not their own. "The spoils system" is a political term. It has been prominent in our politics since the time of Andrew Jackson, whose administration was a paragon of the art of political pork. In government administration, this is, quite simply, the characteristic problem. Not only at the lower rungs, but also at the top, the interest of the government and the governed are difficult to bring into accord. That is why only specific things should be done by government, and then only when specific controls are in place to prevent abuse.

No amount of vigilance can remove the danger entirely. Only constant vigilance can prevent it eating the seed corn of an entire nation, even a rich nation such as ours. That is why C.S. Lewis, in a famous little story about a minor tempter here on Earth and his supervising devil down below, was led to describe Hell—as a bureaucracy.

One may protest that just this kind of graft is common in the larger corporations. For example, IBM employees have recently been found stealing valuable computer boards and selling them for a tiny fraction of their worth. Some items worth $2000 at wholesale were going for $75. One employee was quoted to the effect that this practice is common. If this kind of thing happens in the private sector, why then is Hell only a government—and not also a corporate—bureaucracy?

The answer is that a government bureaucracy and a large corporation have some things in common, but the latter is not so bad as to be hellish. Stealing in IBM, or waste and abuse by its employees, are admittedly much more likely than in the corner grocery store, where the proprietor lives over the shop. *He* would not steal from the store because it belongs to him already. His employees might steal, but he is always watching. IBM is vulnerable to some kinds of abuse, merely because it is *large*.

Yet three things distinguish IBM from the government. The first is sheer size: according to *NPR*, the government of the United States has more than 7 times as many employees as the largest corporation in the country. If size is a problem, Uncle Sam is a behemoth of trouble. Here is a vastness, in administrative sprawl and intricacy, to make the Grand seem a baby canyon, or Everest a hillock.

The second is more to the point. It goes by the name of Apple, and Unisys, and Compaq, and Honeywell, and on and on. These are the competitors of IBM, and every one of them is out to destroy that company and take its place. They impose on IBM swift and hurtful penalties, if for a moment IBM should forget or mistake the interest of its customers.

Just lately, for example, the competitors of IBM have been taking market share at a prodigious rate. IBM, whose name has been a synonym for power and unassailable success, has become in two short years a laughing stock and a victim. Writing off some billions in "restructuring charges," IBM is suddenly in a fight for its life. Its CEO, Mr. Akers, was three years ago the very epitome of corporate establishment. He is now dismissed in ignominy, as is much of his team. A new man is there, and he is cutting everywhere—salaries, positions, bonuses, output. IBM failed to serve its customers. That error is always potentially fatal.

The shareholders who by law are owners of this enterprise and have control of its operations now find that they have, in hard reality, that natural companion of authority—responsibility. At the peak IBM stock sold for upwards of $200 per share. Now it languishes near $50, and its owners are poorer by 75 percent. This is no impostor; this is the real article we call *competition*. In the waging of it, the participants bet their labor and their livelihoods. Defeat is sudden and expensive. It can be complete. There is one way to win this competition (leaving out of account the help of government). That way is to serve customers.

The *NPR* runs on quite a bit about inducing competition within government, and also about organizing the government to serve its customers. We see two problems with this.

The first problem is that competition in government can very seldom be made real. The *NPR* proposes to make agencies "compete" with one another. Right away however it excludes key parts of the bureaucracy:

> Not all federal operations should be forced to compete, of course. Competition between regulatory agencies is a terrible idea. (Witness the regulation of banks, which can decide to charter with the state or federal government, depending on where they can find the most lenient regulations.) Nor should policy agencies compete. In the development of policy, cooperation between different units of government is essential. Competition creates turf wars, which get in the way of creating rational policies and programs. It is in service delivery that competition yields results because competition is the one force that gives public agencies no choice but to improve.

In other words, policy and enforcement will be, if anything, more centralized in the new plan than it has been. If we exclude the regulatory agencies and the policy agencies, we exclude the EPA, which has put a man in jail for cleaning up a dumping ground. We exclude OSHA, which harasses business for the sport of it. We exclude the Department of Interior, which classifies little low places in the ground as "wetlands" and prevents mining that will ultimately replace those low places with lakes. We exclude a lot that is important, to any real system of regulatory relief.

We do still *include* much that is important. We include the Post Office, which ought to be in private hands anyway. We include the welfare agencies, where the fact of the payments, and the way they are calculated and made, is at least as important as how much it costs to make them. We include, in short, a lot of places where people deal with the government because they must, or where people get something from the government for free. Efficiencies in these places, if they can be made, will be welcome, but even if they are made, they do not address the root issue.

That raises the other side of the point about "competing" for "customers." The *NPR* says:

> By "customer," we do not mean "citizen." A citizen can participate in democratic decision making; a customer receives benefits from a specific service. All Americans are citizens. Most are also customers: of the U.S. Postal Service, the Social Security Administration, the Department of Veterans Affairs, the National Park Service, and scores of other federal organizations.
>
> In a democracy, citizens and customers both matter. But when they vote, citizens seldom have much chance to influence the behavior of public institutions that directly affect their lives: schools, hospitals, farm service agencies, social security offices. It is a sad irony: citizens own their government, but private businesses they do not own work much harder to cater to their needs.

This gets near the heart of the problem. Not one of the functions of government listed above—schools, hospitals, farm service agencies, social security offices—would have been considered by James Madison or his colleagues in Philadelphia as a proper function of the national government. They believed that these administrative functions should be private, or when public, locally controlled. The national government, as a whole, must be accountable to its citizens, and it must be accountable to them, *as citizens*.

The *NPR* is worse than merely confused about the proper function of the government; it is at best unconcerned about it. For that reason it seeks not only to mimic the *methods*, but also to appropriate to itself the *ends* that companies serve. The *NPR* defines politics in the well-known Harold Lasswell phrase: "who gets what, when, how." In the American system, where the political institution of property rights[2] give rise to a market system of distributing goods, this function is not actually carried out by government. It is delegated to a vast and competitive market, in which voluntary transactions among customers and suppliers are the staple of trade.

The delegation of this important function was made deliberately in our system, and for good cause. It was made to avoid the dangers inherent in a centralized, public system of allocating economic goods. In their relation to the government, people are not properly "customers," they are "citizens." When large classes of them become customers, their interest in the government is changed. Customers become distinct in society from citizens, and yet they still have the authority of citizenship. In fundamental respects their interests are opposed to citizens who are not customers. Today the two opposing political parties each derive their main strength from one side of this division. The tendency of this division is to convert elections into a contest over money. In that case the rights of minorities are in jeopardy. It is not by accident that we have redefined the term "minority" to mean in fact a favored *majority* of people, who have been qualified as particularly deserving customers of government.

In the end this dispute between citizens and customers about how government should function, points to a dispute about what government should do.

We said the problems with the *NPR* begin with its method and end with its scope. That scope is too confined: "The *National Performance Review* focused primarily on how government should work, not on what it should do" (*NPR*, Preface). Since the beginning of the Progressive Era, the government has increasingly taken the view that it should do more, and ever more. Perhaps the most radical, if not the most profound, statement of the vast ambition of progressive government has been given by the current first lady. She said, at the University of Texas, that she hopes "to change what it means to be a human being in the 21st century." This radical project is a far different thing than the government we had, resting fixed upon the immutable laws of human nature, and meaning to secure to us our liberty and a fair chance. In this radical project, government does not do things *for* us, it does things *to* us.

Consider the danger of this distinction. We said that there were three respects in which IBM is different from the government. We have named two. The last is the most important. The government, dealing with a higher subject matter than the corporation, has greater powers. In the cause of justice the government has the power to command much more than the money of its citizens. It may with justice command them to fight and to die. It may arrest them and restrain their liberty or end their lives.

The example of the U.S. marshals is once again apposite. A case arose lately in Los Angeles in which the county sheriffs suspected a man of growing marijuana in his back garden. They thought they spotted the plants from a helicopter. This man's back garden happened to occupy some fancy real estate near a fine beach, and quite a lot of it. We know that one of the first steps of the sheriffs was to get an appraisal of his house and garden, to find out how much they would get if they could seize them. We know that their budget is tight, and the sheriffs want raises in pay and more help. We know that they went to the man's house and raided it in the middle of the night while he was in bed, and we know that they shot him dead. We know that they found no marijuana.

A county prosecutor formed the view that this was a mercenary raid, undertaken to support the departmental budget. Other and higher officials have disagreed with him. Whether he is right or not, the lesson here is still very clear. The sheriffs had something more than a *duty* to find the marijuana; in this case they had also an *interest*. We need institutions of government that make sure, and then double sure, that officers with guns act in accordance with their duty, and not in accordance with their interest.

Our country is blessed with the finest historic safeguards to protect its citizens from the arbitrary use of power, either by the tax collector, or the regulator, or officers with guns. In the end those safeguards all rely on one that is fundamental— the control of the government by the citizens who own it. According to the *NPR*, citizens today "seldom have much chance to influence the behavior of public institutions that directly affect their lives." This is a drastic problem. It is the problem of government in our time. It will not be repaired—on the contrary—it will exacerbated by a further division of our people into customers and citizens.

The *National Performance Review* is a dangerous document, because it is skillful, or anyway more skillful than is common from presidents today. It seeks, with partial success, to appeal at the same time to two different and usually opposed audiences, to customers of government, and to citizens who pay for it. Behind this document is a political understanding that far surpasses anything in the Carter or the Bush years. Expect from the Clinton administration no public hand wringing or expressions of futility. This administration will not be surprised or appalled by much that it finds while in power. It has thought the problem through.

Our government has reached the sorry point at which it is necessary to think all over again about what it should do. It is time to recover our constitutional legacy of a *limited* government, existing for definite purposes, founded upon clear, true and permanent ideas. Until we get that back, we cannot trust the system. Serious people may therefore prefer that the government waste money rather than use it. The *National Performance Review* may give us the worst of both worlds, a government more costly and more ardent in pursuit of power. Red tape may be our last friend.

Endnotes

1. Remarks by President Clinton at the National Prayer Breakfast, February 4, 1993.

2. For a discussion of the democratic purpose of property rights in the Founding, see Thomas G. West, "Property and the Public Good: The Founder's View," Claremont Institute paper #1992-1, January 8, 1992.

— 7 —

Clinton's New Citizenship

Charles E. Parton

America is a nation in transition. The end of the Cold War closes a long chapter in the history of our country, and the chapter on post-Cold War America has yet to be written. The opportunity to define the agenda for the 90s and beyond completely escaped the Bush administration, leaving the first pages of our new history to be written by President Bill Clinton. It is a chapter that will record an unprecedented ideological and political victory for the liberal agenda.

Less than one year into the Clinton presidency, it has become apparent that one would be foolhardy to make predictions as to the intentions, or the capabilities, of this adminstration. Yet, the task seems so necessary. Projecting the consequences of the Clinton victory grows more complex as the president continues to search for his core, and both foreign and domestic policy await that great day when it reveals itself. To date, his convictions seem somewhat malleable, and even whimsical. Meanwhile, both the domestic and the international community languish in discomfort, awaiting some sign that this administration is capable of providing a reasonable level of statemanship to the world. If we have already seen the best of Clinton's leadership, surely voters will reject his second offering if they are given a viable alternative.

Few pundits, however, would have predicted during the early primaries that Clinton would be the Democratic nominee for president in '92, and even fewer would have predicted him to be in the Oval Office without an invitation. Once elected, few would have guessed that the so called honeymoon period would be one of such turmoil, and once past, even fewer would have predicted that he could reconcile his administrative disaster in time to pass an unpopular tax package through an unwilling Congress—but he has.

Clinton's electoral success depended on his ability to convince 43 percent of the voting public on two essential points. First, with a cavalier disregard for the truth, he assaulted the record of the Reagan presidency, and at least some voters were willing to agree with his repeated assertion that the Reagan/Bush years were twelve years of failure. Second, he was able to convince voters that he was a "new Democrat," all the while failing to define what that really meant.

The problem with politics is politicians. I'm not referring to the honest and dedicated individuals that elect to serve the public, but rather to the political hacks that abuse both the voters and the offices they obtain. They are a class of people unto themselves, willing to do and say whatever it takes to be elected. They corrupt the system in every way, serving themselves instead of the public. The disease is bi-partisan, but Bill Clinton personifies it with the best of them.

During the campaign, George Bush warned us that Clinton would impose a huge tax increase on the American public.

Clinton denied it. Bush warned the public that Clinton had developed a "pattern of deceit," to "watch out for your wallet," and he warned us that Clinton would be inept at foreign policy. Bush also accurately predicted that Clinton would waffle on important issues. And he challenged Bill Clinton's claim of centrism. George Bush was correct in each of his assertions and warnings, and Bill Clinton did and said whatever he needed to in order to get elected.

From the outset, Clinton realized that in order to win the Oval Office he would have to recapture the Reagan Democrats. There would be no future in Washington for the typical Democratic dove, devoid of determination to maintain a strong military and a strong foreign policy. Clinton praised the democrats of the former Soviet Union, damned the Chinese Communists and pledged military support for Bosnia. Conservative Democrats have generally endorsed a strong military, recognizing the wisdom of the peace-through-strength doctrine. They now realize that the chance they took on Clinton being a moderate is a lost cause.

So exactly how consequential is the Clinton victory? It is not only consequential for the conservative Democrats, but the nation as a whole. For left-wing liberals, the Clinton victory is a great victory. They can now proceed, unencumbered, with the socialization of America, and they will be led by Hillary Clinton. Bill wasn't kidding when, during the campaign, he said you get two for the price of one. Bill gets to be president, and Hillary gets to run the country. For them, reality is better than a dream.

When we attempt to measure the success of a presidency, we should measure the actions of the administration against the expectations of the electorate. Such an evaluation becomes exceedingly difficult in the case of the Clinton administration.

It is difficult because Clinton won the election by a plurality, leaving obscure the intentions of the majority. And it is difficult because Clinton deceived the electorate by distorting the political accomplishments of his past, as well as the intentions of his coming presidency. If he had announced during the campaign that he intended to impose a 300 billion dollar tax increase to accompany his 200 billion dollar budget deficit, he would not have been elected. I suspect that neither Clinton nor the electorate really know what to expect of each other

What should reasonable people expect from their government? Ignore for the moment the definition of Republican or Democratic expectations, and try to formulate for yourself what you would reasonably expect from your government when you live in a thriving nation of people whose commonalities are exceedingly greater than their differences. Decide for yourself the reasonable expectations of a reasonable people.

We could reasonably expect that, if we are the producing element of a free-market economy, we are making a positive contribution to society, and, doing no harm to others, we should be encouraged to keep up the good work. If that society is enjoying the highest standard of living in the world, one would reasonably conclude that the system is working and should be perpetuated. If that is our expectation, how does the Clinton tax increase, gays in the military and the destruction of the best health care system in the world contribute to that?

We could reasonably expect that attempts to change a prosperous economic system, one that has produced the highest living standard in the world, led and financed the free world to a victory over the most oppressive regimes of our time, and proven itself to be the most charitable of all societies, would be thwarted with a vengence. If that is our expectation, how does the nationalization of 15 percent of the national economy contribute?

One could reasonably expect that, above all else, the respect for individual liberty would thrive in a free society. How does progressive taxation, packaged as retribution for success, square with the protection of property rights?

It is a consequence of the Clinton victory in 1992 that it is no longer practical to have reasonable expectations. The Clinton agenda is not one of economic growth, but one of economic redistribution, and a declared war on constitutional democracy.

> A democracy cannot exist as a permanent form of government. It can only exist until the voters discover that they can vote themselves a largess from the treasury. From that moment on, the majority will always vote for the candidates promising the most benefits from the public treasury, with the result that a democracy always collapses over loose fiscal policy. (Alexander Tyler, circa 1775)

Since the New Deal, essentially the last sixty years, politicians from both parties have taken extraordinary liberties with the public treasury. The Clinton agenda, however, institutionalizes the idea that the purpose of government is to take the assets of one class in order to create "security" for other classes. The Clinton tax-package, National Health Care Reform, Family Leave, and National Service all depend on the redistribution of assets to create equality of outcome. Incidentally, it is no accident that the supposed benefits of many of these programs do not begin until his second term, essentially financing his re-election bid from the public trough.

The nation might well benefit if the president declared a temporary hiatus from the campaign trail.

In the process, it is Clinton's intention to redefine the purpose of government, rejecting entirely the constitutional edifice of the Founding Fathers, in addition to rejecting the principles themselves. The sequence of events deriving predominantly from the programs instituted during the New Deal have already altered to a great extent the American understanding of the purpose of government. James Madison's understanding was that this government was created for the protection of individual liberty, and that the protection of individual liberty was manifested in the right to own property. In order to "reinvent government" according to his own vision, Clinton must reject the principles of the Founding, which he has done. He must contend that private property is harmful to the public good, and he does so by demanding progressive taxation for the purposes of redistribution, and by the excessive regulations that restrict productive utilization of private land.

According to the Founding Fathers, the right to own property transcended the creation of wealth; it established limitations on government. Appropriately, our Constitution was written in anticipation of Bill Clinton's election; written to defy any assertion that our Constitution, and the principles defined therein, was only a list of suggestions. The right to own property was meant to provide protection for the gains obtained from one's industry and merit. It was acknowledged that not all men would be inclined to produce at the same level, that some were more capable than others or some were more ambitious than others. The first purpose of government, according to Madison, was to protect the diverse and unequal faculties of men for acquiring property. Each man should be encouraged to pursue his interests in an effort to become a self-reliant citizen. For the republic to succeed it would be necessary for the more capable of its citizens to participate, and such participation would not occur if their individual efforts were not rewarded, and if the fruits of their labor were not protected.

Under the Clinton leadership, Senator Patrick Moynihan proudly proclaims the Clinton tax package to be the most progressive he has ever seen. Madison would interpret that statement to mean that the tax package is the most un-American proposal he has ever seen. Progressive taxation is a rejection of "the diversity of faculties" premise, and a contention that no citizen has the right to succeed above the limitations set by the government. The Clinton agenda announces, for all to hear, that property rights, and, therefore, individual liberty, will be meted out by the government rather than protected by the U.S. Constitution.

Hillary Clinton, speaking to a group of medical students, put the opponents of the nanny state on notice when she proclaimed that it is time to put the common good, the national interest, ahead of the individual. To the Clintons, however, "the common good," "the national interest," is not the Madisonian model that insists that the community was established for the purpose of protecting the rights of the individual. To them, "the common good" means the state. To Madison, justice is the common good, the core of which is the protection of the rights of the individual.

The distorted view that the Clintons hold as to what is best for America is reflected in their advocacy for gay rights, and in their plans for the redistribution of the wealth of the nation. Was there really a mandate for the appointment of gays and lesbians to the Cabinet? Was there a national clamor for opening the military to some grand social experiment in alternative lifestyles? Was there a consensus that the purpose of government was to create a new and exclusive set of rights for gay and lesbian couples? And is it true that Americans wanted our new president to seek some sort of retribution against those citizens that had financial success in the 1980s? That these are the positions held by the Clinton regime is another confirmation that they stand outside the mainstream understanding of the purpose of government.

The Clinton Presidency will fail for two reasons. It demands new definitions of justice and equality that reject the Madisonian common good. The Clinton principle asserts that justice means economic equality between all men. It further advocates that it is the role of government to create economic equality. It will never happen in a free society. Men have the right to succeed, to produce and to profit from their labor. "And inasmuch as most good things are produced by labor, it follows that all such things of right belongs to those whose labor has produced them . . . To secure to each laborer the whole product of his labor, or as nearly as possible, is a worthy object of any good government." (Abraham Lincoln, Dec. 1, 1847)

And, though not as rhetorically attractive, men have the right to fail. What is called opportunity, or entrepreneurship, is having the courage to risk success and failure. It is not only what drives the American economy, but is the basis of citizenship. Justice requires that there should exist some penalty for failure, and rewards for success. Americans understand it, and wouldn't have it any other way. They cherish the idea of creating wealth because of the good it brings and because of the character it demands. Keeping the doors of opportunity open is the real national interest and the best way to serve the common good.

While the government can play a constructive role in helping to improve the lives of the disadvantaged, such actions must take place within the context of the Madisonian constitutional limits on government; removing obstacles to success rather than providing for dependency. There are few problems that Americans face today that could not be solved if good jobs were available. Excessive taxation and regulation, the products of intrusive government, have eliminated those jobs. Clinton's vision is of the Supreme State, a fantasyland in which government cures all ills through a doctrine of economic parity. In realityland, it becomes a roadblock to opportunity. Clinton's fantasyland, and the reality of what it means to be an American, are two parallel universes, co-existing without relationship to each other.

If one's purpose is to narrow the gap between the poor and the wealthy, certain conditions must prevail. There can be no incentive to acquire property that is not accompanied by a guarantee that such property will be protected once acquired. The protection of property that is provided must apply equally, to those who own substantial property, and to those who own little.

> Property is the fruit of labor—property is desirable—is a positive good in the world. That some should be rich, shows that others may become rich, and hence is just encouragement to industry and enterprize. Let not him who is houseless pull down the house of another; but let him labor diligently and build one for himself, thus by example assuring that his own shall be safe from violence when built. (Abraham Lincoln, March 21, 1864)

There is no room in this equation for governmental redistribution of property. Clinton will fail for the same reason that liberalism fails; it seeks justice for the poor while denying justice to the wealthy. In a free society, justice must exist for all. That is the true basis for community.

In reality, the attempt to create economic "security" through perverted principles creates a widening of the gap between rich and poor. Liberalism seeks to redistribute the economic pie rather than to grow the pie, and the pie can grow larger only when value is added into the economic pie mix. As those with fresh capital invest in the economy, the economy grows and the poor can benefit. When government grows, it does so by taking capital out of the economy; the economy shrinks and the poor fail to benefit.

The anticipated success of the New Deal, the Great Society and the War on Poverty has long been dispelled, and yet, the financial burden of these failed programs remain. The same Americans that risked their lives abroad, fighting Communism and Fascism, ardently support the collectivism of Social Security and welfare and appear to lend support to the lure of socialized medicine. Ironically, if asked to abandon our constitutional form of government for a form of socialism, these same recipients would readily take up arms in patriotic resistance. This contradiction of values is the national vice. The simultaneous demand for individual liberty and governmentally administered security, which must depend on the confiscation of the property of others, lacks rationality. It has been the philosophy of the Clinton administration to exploit the national vice to its fullest political advantage.

The best description of the state of the nation under Bill Clinton is "chaos." Even his most ardent supporters must have been startled when he announced, less than three weeks into his administration, that he had reduced interest rates and created thousands of new jobs. His politics are of expediency. He is the worst kind of politician. Clinton's desire to be president is not based on a desire to serve the nation, but, rather, a need to serve his personal arrogance. His is a presidency that rejects the principles of the Founding in the attempt to reinvent a government that is not "of the people, by the people, for the people," but above the people. In Clinton's new order we will take no pride in being self-reliant, in being independent, because it will no longer be a requirement of citizenship that we be so. Bill Clinton will feel our pain, and he will take care of us. Bill Clinton is always ready to proclaim himself as the guardian of security and fairness, ignoring that our only real security lies in our ability to provide for ourselves. I have never heard him mention the U.S. Constitution as the protector of rights.

The principles that define our national character have been written into a Constitution that, for over 200 years, has acted as a sentry against the invasion of individual liberty and guarded us against the perversion of self-government. We are, after all, a nation of principles, and our Constitution was written so that we might refer to those principles, and not forget them. The Constitution stands between the declaration of a people to remain free, and the totalitarian inclinations of a government too powerful and too committed to its own will to honor its intended purpose. Bill Clinton can create no rights or create no protections that are not already secured by the Constitution. The sooner he realizes it, the sooner David Gergen can remove the training wheels from the presidency.

— 8 —

Foreign Policy as Economic Security

Patrick J. Garrity

After its first year in office, the Clinton administration has begun to develop a vision of American interests and American foreign policy in the post-Cold War world. The operational logic of that vision can be characterized briefly as follows: (1) President Clinton has made jobs, and specifically the creation of high-paying, skilled jobs, the centerpiece of his administration; (2) these jobs can best, and largely, be created through international trade; (3) increased American exports requires both improved American competitiveness (which sets the administration's domestic agenda) and assured access to foreign markets; (4) obtaining access to foreign markets and advantageous conditions for American trade requires continued U.S. global leadership; albeit at reduced cost; and (5) to pursue its vision of a new world economic order, the administration must find ways to prevent or manage regional security crises so that it can focus its energies, and the attention of the American public, on what truly matters: jobs, jobs, jobs.

Clinton's vision of the emerging world turns on its head the logic of American policy during the Cold War. National security was then defined fundamentally in political-military terms ("high politics"): preventing the strategic expansion of the Soviet Union. Once this first and necessary condition for Western security was achieved, the nation could then pay attention to pursuing its international economic goals ("low politics").[1] The Clinton administration, by contrast, adopts the assumptions of the "economics first" school of international politics, of whom Paul Kennedy is perhaps the most prominent member. The president would elevate American economic interests to the pride of place in U.S. foreign policy, while subordinating the traditional political-military dimension to a supporting role.

In evaluating the Clinton administration's foreign policy, most outside observers have tended to focus on the administration's difficulty in articulating any sort of coherent approach to the world—and especially its operational incompetence in managing crises in the Balkans, Somalia, and Haiti. Such inarticulateness and incompetence is not a trivial concern, as we will discuss later. But by late 1993, the outlines of a serious and reasonably coherent administration policy had begun to emerge, which analysts should take great care to understand and evaluate on its own terms. That is the approach of this essay. We conclude in the end that the administration may lack the leverage and opportunity to realize its political economic goals, however clever they may be in concept, unless substantial adjustments to the realities of international relations and domestic politics are made.

TOWARD A NEW WORLD ECONOMIC ORDER

President Clinton and his advisers have frequently proclaimed that the emergence of an integrated global economy is one of the defining characteristics of the post-Cold War world—and quite possibly the most important. With the disappearance of Soviet communism, the most pressing challenge to American well-being comes not from direct military threats but, it is said, from economic competitors in Europe and Asia. The central object of the administration, in both its foreign and domestic policy components, is to improve the competitiveness of American industry and, specifically, the American worker. Failure to do so will result in a shrinking standard of living for ordinary Americans and a permanent decline in the global economic, political, and military status of the United States.

To avoid decline, the administration proposes first and foremost to address deficiencies in American economy and society that have supposedly hampered competitiveness. This involves reducing the federal budget deficit while increasing government spending in so-called investment accounts, which are said to be sources of long-term growth in productivity— e.g., infrastructure, education, and research and development. Further, the administration argues that it will be necessary to increase the "security" of the American worker, and especially the middle class, in order to provide them with the confidence to take the personal risks necessary to become fully competitive in the world market. These domestic security programs include universal health care, job retraining programs, and anti-crime legislation.

Whether the Clinton domestic agenda will achieve its goals of increasing American competitiveness and improving the standard of living is a subject addressed by other authors in this volume. For our purposes, we would note that there is, in theory, a seamless web between the Clinton administration's foreign and domestic policy. Clinton advisers point out that exports have accounted for the greater part of U.S. economic growth since the late 1980s, and that exports tend to provide higher-paying jobs than industries that only serve the domestic market. To continue an export-driven economic strategy, the administration must not only increase the relative performance of American industries and workers with respect to foreign competitors; it must also ensure access to foreign markets. The administration accordingly has to make a concerted effort to promote U.S. exports wherever and however possible, whether through multilateral agreements on trade liberalization; unilateral pressure against what the administration considers unfair trade barriers to U.S. goods and services; or direct U.S. government assistance to American firms doing business abroad.

The Clinton administration believes that continued American international leadership is necessary to ensure that foreign markets remain or become open. Without energetic American policies, political forces in Europe and Asia will tend toward protectionism, potentially leaving the United States economically isolated in the Western Hemisphere in a world divided into exclusive and hostile regional trading blocs. But the administration does not believe that the United States enjoys the same absolute power that it did during the Cold War, because of the growth of the economies of many other nations. Accordingly, President Clinton seeks to find ways to leverage the United States' unique assets to increase relative American power in the short term, while relying on the revitalization of the U.S. economy to provide the long-term foundation for the domestic renewal of America (and its continued international predominance).

The first leverage point for the United States is its ability to play one region off against another for American economic advantage. Thus, Congressional approval of NAFTA (the North American Free Trade Agreement) in November provided Clinton with political leverage in the subsequent APEC (Asia Pacific Economic Cooperation forum) meeting in Seattle, as he sought to open Asian, and specifically Japanese, markets. The apparently successful APEC meeting, in turn, provided Clinton with a stronger hand against the Europeans in his efforts to bring the Uruguay round of the GATT (General Agreement on Trade and Tariffs) talks to a successful conclusion. This policy of economic maneuvering does not however imply an equality of priority among the regions. The administration appears to believe that Europe is a region in economic decline, with relatively limited opportunities for American trade and investment as compared with Asia. By some estimates, the overall growth rate in Asia for 1992 was 7.8 percent, compared with a 1.1 percent figure for Europe (the North American growth rate was 2.1 percent). Turning towards Asia as a source of dynamism for the American economy would logically lead the United States to reorient its alliance relationships, military force structure, and the like to accommodate an Asia-first policy—reversing the strategic priorities of the past 50 years.

The second point of leverage likewise reflects an attempt to reverse the patterns of the Cold War. When the U.S.-Soviet competition dominated the concerns of American policy makers, the United States made economic concessions to its allies in order to gain their cooperation on security matters. The Clinton administration now seeks allied accommodation on trade issues as a *quid pro quo* for continued American security guarantees—which guarantees presumably remain of sufficient importance to the allies that they will make economic concessions to Washington.

The third point of leverage is to use multilateral instruments of security to reduce the burdens on the U.S. military, permitting the United States to decrease its defense expenditures safely and redirect the savings into domestic investment accounts and deficit reduction. The United Nations is supposed to take the lead in what the administration terms "humanitarian" military interventions, while the United States retains the capability to act, unilaterally if necessary, in defense of its "vital" interests.

This leads to the fourth, and perhaps most critical element of the Clinton administration's search for foreign policy leverage: preventive diplomacy. In principle, the administration seeks to defuse or manage potential regional crises diplomatically before they reach the stage where they distract the president and the American public from their quest for economic security. In practice, this means gambling to some extent that the world will remain sufficiently quiet for the next several years so as to allow the president to implement his domestic and international economic agendas, and for new regional security arrangements to emerge that will serve to dampen conflict over the longer term. The administration's stance towards North Korea's nuclear program—tough public rhetoric, but reluctance to force any sort of confrontation—is one example of preventive diplomacy in action. The United States has also made the decision to throw its lot in with Russian President Boris Yeltsin, in hopes that democratic and market reform will solidify a pro-Western foreign policy for the Russian Federation. Such a positive outcome in Moscow would prevent what the administration defines as the greatest potential short-term threat to American security, and to Clinton's economic-centered foreign policy: that is, a newly aggressive Russia determined to oppose American regional interests in Eurasia. A key part of Clinton's strategy to buttress Yeltsin's position is effectively to allow Russia a relatively free hand in dealing with what the Russians call the "near abroad"—the other former Soviet republics (except for the Baltic states, at least at the moment), including Ukraine. The Clinton administration is also resisting efforts to expand NATO membership eastward, on the grounds that this would be regarded as a threatening development by Moscow. Such consideration of Russia's interests, it is hoped, will strengthen Yeltsin's hands against hard-line nationalist elements in Russia, while buying time for Russian reform to take hold.

To succeed in his effort to recast American foreign policy, President Clinton must establish a workable popular and Congressional consensus behind a new kind of American internationalism. The president and other administration officials have understood since the beginning that continued American global engagement and leadership (especially in its political and military dimensions) has been under attack from both the right and the left. Until recently, administration officials have struggled to mount a coherent defense of internationalism, and they have been hampered by the fact that the president preferred to focus on the domestic elements of his strategy of economic revitalization. But the NAFTA debate clearly energized Clinton and allowed him, intellectually and politically, to make the link between American economic growth and U.S. interests abroad. This linkage permits the administration to justify international engagement and leadership to the American public as the central mechanism to create high-paying jobs in the United States. Hence, the administration increasingly views foreign and military policy issues according to their impact on our trade objectives, which objectives in turn will be driven by an assessment of how trade can best support the domestic economy.

HOW TO THINK ABOUT THE CLINTON FOREIGN POLICY

If President Clinton can realize the vision outlined above, he will have gone far in improving American economic and military security at less cost than that required to wage the Cold War. Whether he will be able to realize such a vision, in whole or in part, depends critically on whether the leverage points noted above do in fact exist. It also depends on the operational competence of the administration, domestically and internationally, to take advantage of that supposed leverage. Reasonable doubts exist on both accounts.

With respect to the question of leverage, it remains to be demonstrated that other major powers, including Japan and Germany, will accept American global economic leadership on Clinton's terms, or that they will be willing to pay (in terms of significant trade concessions) for the privilege of an American security guarantee. To be sure, American leadership and military protection is welcomed, or at least accepted, by many key nations. But with the end of the Cold War threat and the economic emergence of Europe (if temporarily lagging) and Asia, these nations are beginning to develop their own distinct political and strategic interests. There is a point at which American hectoring on economics—and especially implicit threats to remove the U.S. security umbrella—may lead to a break in political relations rather than a strengthening of the American economic position.[2] Tokyo and Berlin, among others, now have options to operate independently of Washington that they did not previously possess, however reluctant they may be to exercise those options. To be sure, the United

States should not neglect its economic interests or its unique position of international leadership, but it must develop a new style of leadership that accommodates the legitimate interests of others.

This cautionary point raises a deeper issue: whether the Clinton administration's "economy first" approach prematurely discounts the geopolitical dimensions of international relations. There is certainly no guarantee that ambitious or desperate regional powers, such as North Korea or Serbia, will elect to remain passive over the next five years while the administration puts the American economic house in order. The implicit U.S. approach toward Russia—not opposing Moscow in its ambitions to reestablish predominance over the territory of the former Soviet Union—is a particularly critical gamble. Arguably, an imperial Russia cannot also be a liberal Russia, and by implicitly condoning the former the administration is inadvertently sabotaging the latter.[3] Also, there is no guarantee that Russian imperialism would stop with a *de facto* restoration of the former Soviet Union. The countries of east-central Europe are already deeply concerned about a new wave of Russian imperialism, which accounts for their urgent desire to begin the process of acquiring membership in NATO. To date, the administration appears to be bowing to Russian pressure to keep these countries out of NATO, but the desirability of giving any government in Moscow an effective veto over Western security interests in the heart of Europe is a dubious policy at best.[4] In addition, the administration appears not to be giving sufficient consideration to an equally significant geopolitical event: the possibility that the Russian Federation, like the Soviet Union, might wholly or partially disintegrate. The American focus on the center (Moscow) thus may lead to missed opportunities to develop a better understanding of, and contacts in, the various regions of Russia.

It is also far from clear that the administration can safely reduce the burdens of the U.S. global military superpower status without jeopardizing its larger political-economic ambitions. The limitations of relying on the United Nations for relief have become so obvious as not to require comment. The Defense Department's recent Bottom Up Review claimed that, despite reductions in defense spending, the United States itself will still be capable of fighting and winning two nearly simultaneous regional wars (e.g., against Iraq and North Korea). Most serious military analysts outside the administration challenge this assumption. The U.S. military is already stretched thin with its various peacekeeping and forward presence commitments. Senate Armed Services Committee Chairman Sam Nunn, along with several members of the Joint Chiefs of Staff, have publicly signaled their concern that U.S. military capability and readiness are already on the ragged edge—even before the administration imposes deeper defense cuts than those now projected (which additional cuts seem almost certain to be made). To be sure, if all remains reasonably quiet on the international scene, this reduction in military capability might never become evident. But continued poor American performances in peacekeeping operations such as Somalia, much less a major setback in a future Operation Desert Storm, would have a devastating impact on the United States' international prestige and cause current allies, greater and lesser, to seek other means of security. This would undermine the administration's efforts to create and lead a new world economic order, and perhaps lead to the marginalization of American political-military influence in key regions, especially Europe.

One should also question the administration's ability to translate its vision of a new economic order into continued public support for American international engagement. Historically, a focus on international economics has appealed to isolationist rather than internationalist sentiment. Recall George Washington's formulation in the Farewell Address: "The great rule of conduct for us in regard to foreign nations is, in extending our commercial relations to have with them as little *political* connection as possible." Washington's rule made perfect sense for the United States in the context of the late 18th century, but it later became an unthinking dictum of those who failed to recognize that economic interests, as well as other interests, can generate overseas political commitments that do require military defense. Latter-day isolationists are certain to renew the claim that, with the collapse of the Soviet threat, the United States can return to an "economy first and only" foreign policy. Clinton's rhetoric runs the danger of reinforcing rather than countering that sentiment. The genius of U.S. post-Cold War internationalism was that it combined moral and geopolitical concerns—the need to contain the Soviet Union—with the legitimate promotion of U.S. economic interests. This formulation appealed successfully to the enlightened self-interest of the American people. It remains to be seen whether Clinton's rather crass appeal to "jobs, jobs, jobs" is alone sufficient to command the better instincts of the American people and overcome their natural and understandable desire to turn inward.

Arguably, in international relations, a well-executed plan of questionable merit is superior to a noble effort badly done. Setting aside the merits of Clinton's econo-centric approach to the world, we are therefore entitled to inquire about the operational competence of the administration. Here there are considerable grounds for concern, especially since the administration relies so heavily on the effective prevention and management of regional crises to free up time and resources for promoting the new American economic agenda. The Clinton administration's foreign policy team contains many of the same individuals who served in the Carter administration. This in itself is not undesirable, as many of these officials served previously with distinction, and experience does count. Still, the Clinton administration's inept execution of policy in situations such as Bosnia, Somalia and Haiti has shown distressing similarities to that of the failed Carter presidency. President Clinton has chosen to dismiss the significance of these "secondary" mistakes and to emphasize the operational success of "primary" efforts such as NAFTA, APEC, and support for Russian reform. But this ignores the fact that failures to deal with crises that the administration attempts to define as being peripheral to American interests can easily lead to a more general erosion of domestic and international confidence. This is precisely what the Iranian hostage crisis did to Jimmy Carter.

Here, responsibility resides at the top. Nothing much happens in this administration without the president's close and careful attention. President Clinton to date has been largely disinterested in foreign affairs, except for those topics dealing directly with American economic security (the Russian problem being defined largely in those terms). If President Clinton is right, if economic matters now control and transcend geopolitical considerations, this lack of attention is proper and salutary. If he is not, then he, and we, will suffer on both accounts.

Endnotes

1.   Revisionist historians argue that American policy makers created and exaggerated the Soviet threat in order to justify U.S. efforts to achieve global economic hegemony. In fact, in its most sophisticated versions, the American strategy of containment assumed that the political-military and political-economic dimensions of U.S. national security policy were intertwined: by promoting stronger economies in the West through increased international trade and cooperation, Washington and its allies would be in a much better position to deal with the Soviet Union. Ironically, the Clinton approach to foreign policy fits the revisionist explanation of American foreign policy more closely than did American policy during the Cold War.

2.   Perhaps the most worrisome situation would be one in which the breakdown of international economic cooperation would lead to a global depression, setting the stage for the revival of great power conflicts as occurred during the 1930s.

3.   In fairness, it should be noted that the American policy of appeasing Moscow with respect to the "near abroad" began in the Bush administration, especially with respect to the disposition of nuclear weapons in Ukraine.

4.   There are also other reasons for hesitating about NATO membership for the East Europeans, such as not wanting to be drawn into a potential morass of ethnic rivalries, but the Russian issue seems to be the dominant one in administration councils.

— 9 —

Clintonism and the Great Leap Forward

C. Bradley Thompson

Speaking for myself, I too believe that humanity will win in the long run. I am only afraid that at some time the world will have turned into one huge hospital where everyone is everybody else's humane nurse.—*Goethe*

Mark 1993 as an ominous turning point in the history of America. This was the year that Franklin Delano Roosevelt's New Deal was finally completed, some sixty years after it was first launched. The Striker Replacement and Family Leave Bills and the Clinton's proposed Health Care Plan represent the last few building blocks needed to complete FDR's blueprint for an American welfare state.

As a consequence of FDR's ultimate victory, the liberalism of our Founding Fathers, the traditional American respect for reason, individualism, property rights, limited government and market capitalism, may now be officially laid to rest. All the principles, symbols, values and virtues that were once instinctual and thought peculiar to Americans are long gone.

And with their loss comes a fundamental change in the nature of what it means to be an American citizen. The American soul has been transformed in some fundamental and important way.

In the eighteenth and nineteenth centuries, there was little government in America relative to the other countries of the developed world. Government in the United States before the First War was lilliputian compared with today. There was very little government at the federal level, and indeed, very little even at the state level. Instead, there was a radical implosion of political power at the local level.

Government in America before the New Deal and certainly before the Civil War had limited power to do things: its primary responsibility was to protect the nation from foreign invasion, to preserve the peace and to adjudicate disputes between citizens. Much beyond that it dared not go. It was a common expression in the eighteenth and nineteenth centuries that those governments which ruled least, ruled best. The Founding Fathers began with the premise that the individual was sovereign and that he must be left free in order to prosper materially and spiritually. Thomas Jefferson said it best when he wrote that the sum of good government was "a wise and frugal government, which shall restrain men from injuring one another, which shall leave them otherwise free to regulate their own pursuits of industry and improvement, and shall not take from the mouth of labor the bread it has earned."

But the Founding generation also knew that the system that promoted individual liberty and the acquisitive spirit was also the system that best fostered responsibility and community. It should not surprise us to learn, then, that the American community was much stronger in the nineteenth century than it is today. There was much less government and a great deal more of civilized society. Political power was weak, but social authority was strong. Communities were thought to be self-governing principally because individuals were self-governing.

During this period of American self-government most institutions or services that we today consider absolutely necessary—hospitals, fire departments, nursing homes, asylums, road building and maintenance, poor relief, etc.—were provided for by voluntary associations. Churches, fraternal organizations, neighbors, families and various charitable organizations took care of the poor and indigent, for instance. Private charity prodded recipients to get back on their feet again as quickly as possible; it was conditional on the recipients working for their assistance; it often demanded that recipients accept certain moral responsibilities; and finally, it made a distinction between the "deserving" and "undeserving" poor, between those who could not help themselves and those who could.

The America of today, however, is an entirely different place. In our brave new world the average American is ruled. The kind of democratic citizen that Benjamin Franklin projected in his *Autobiography* and that Tocqueville described in his *Democracy in America* has been replaced by a new kind of citizen. No longer are Americans thought to be independent and self-governing. Indeed, at times, they seem utterly incapable of self-government. When and how did this great transformation take place?

Culturally and politically, it was the construction and institutionalization of FDR's New Deal that represented the turning point in America's long march away from the moral ideals and political principles of the Founding Fathers. For the first time, the average man was tempted and ultimately seduced by the ideology of collectivism and the promises and favors of the new leviathan state. The nation, declared FDR in his First Inaugural Address, must act "as a trained and loyal army willing to sacrifice for the good of the common discipline."

At the heart of the New Deal was the philosophy of egalitarianism and a radical redefinition of the traditional American notion of "rights." "Rights," as understood by the Founders, meant that all individuals were equally free to pursue and to keep the fruits of their labors. FDR and his New Dealers rejected the Founders' notion of rights. "Everyman has a right to life," said President Roosevelt in his famous Commonwealth Club Address, "and this means that he has also a right to make a comfortable living." It was the responsibility of the state, therefore, to provide security, food, shelter and jobs for all citizens who needed them.

Thus began the massive expansion of the national government in America. The 1930s were a cultural watershed in America's transition from a nation of independent and self-governing citizens to a nation of servile dependents. All Americans, to one degree or another, would now be wards of the state. Today, as a consequence of the New Deal, almost all Americans, including the middle class, live off of some kind of unearned income.

The science-fiction writer Isaac Asimov, writing about life in America in the early part of this century as a newly-arrived immigrant, captured beautifully the old meaning of freedom and its relationship to virtue:

> Everyone faces adversity from time to time. It's a natural part of life. By itself, it's neither good, nor bad. The important thing is how we deal with it and what we learn from it . . .

> Very early in life, poverty forced me to become quick,
> resourceful, and imaginative. It also forced me to accept
> jobs I really didn't want but which helped me grow.

So different is the world of modern America. In the days of pre-New Deal America poverty meant opportunity and opportunity meant freedom and freedom meant living according to certain virtues. Today poverty means entitlements and entitlements mean dependence and dependence means slavery.

The most obvious and distressing example of the way that America has changed is the creation of a black underclass utterly dependent on the state for its survival. There is of course a foul irony in the way in which the bureaucratic-welfare state has so invidiously corrupted the soul of black folk and destroyed the black community in so many of our major cities. Under the old form of slavery, the body was enslaved but the moral spirit was free. Under the new slavery, the body is free but the soul is enslaved to government handouts.

But this turn of soul is not restricted to the black underclass—not by a long shot. It affects all classes, all races, all Americans. The social theorist, Charles Murray, has written brilliantly recently about an alarming new trend in the country: the rapid growth of an alienated and dispossessed white underclass. William Bennett, in his *Index of Leading Cultural Indicators*, has charted America's moral and social decline over the last thirty years, and the results are alarming. Violent crime in this country has increased 560 percent, illegitimate births increased by more than 400 percent, the divorce rate quadrupled, there was a tripling of children living in single-parent homes, and SAT scores dropped by 80 points. The correlation between the rise of the state in the twentieth century and the decline in moral standards is direct and beyond dispute.

Despite the tragic consequences that have attended the growth of the state in modern America, this is not the end of our great twentieth-century experiment in social engineering. For the Clintons, this is the beginning of a new era. The New Deal was not enough, not nearly enough. The American people want "change," say the Clintons, which they interpret as a mandate to revolutionize America's moral, cultural, economic and political life.

America is sick according to Mrs. Clinton. We suffer from an overwhelming sense of meaninglessness. The officially sanctioned "greed" of the Reagan '80s left our souls hollow and unsatisfied. The decade of Reaganism was our decade of meaninglessness.

What the American people desperately need to cure their existential malady, according to Mrs. Clinton, is a new kind of politics—a "politics of meaning." The first lady is calling for nothing less than a Cultural Revolution.

But what could she mean by the politics of meaning? In an extraordinary essay entitled "Saint Hillary" (the article was accompanied by a cover-page illustration of the First Lady shown with robe and crucifix as if to suggest that she is a post-modern Joan of Arc), Michael Kelley of the *New York Times* reports that Mrs. Clinton "is searching for not merely pro-grammatic answers but for The Answer."

We are told that the first lady is "trying to come up with a sort of unified-field theory of life," and that the search of the world's first philosopher-queen is on the order of a total moral "Reformation." According to the *N.Y Times*, Mrs. Clinton has apparently ascended to some kind of higher consciousness, to an exalted plane of moral perfection. The *Washington Post* has endorsed this view of the first lady as well: "She has goals, but they appear to be so huge and far-off—grand and noble things twinkling in the distance—that it's hard to see what she sees." For some, Mrs. Clinton has become a kind of high priestess, a visionary, a moral Einstein who has seen the Light while the rest of us live in the dark cave that we call America.

Let's take a closer look at what she and her intellectual gurus have actually said about the "politics of meaning."

In her now infamous speech at the University of Texas, the first lady called for a national spiritual renewal. The New Deal must be followed by a New Age. "Let us be willing," Mrs. Clinton implored, "to remold society by redefining what it means to be a human being in the 20th century, moving into a new millennium." She implored her audience to merge their separate lives with others as "part of some greater effort." She reminded us that "we are connected to one another," that "we are part of something bigger than ourselves." Such a moral reformation will not be easy, she said. "It's not going to be easy redefining who we are as human beings in this postmodern age." It certainly won't! But surely this kind of sophomoric, late-night, dorm-room existentialism stretches the limits of incredulity when uttered by a grown woman who wants to be in charge of our $850 billion health-care industry.

In a speech to the Association of Medical Colleges, the first lady announced the moral imperative of Clintonism: "It's about time we start thinking about the common good and the national interest, instead of just individuals," she said. Mrs. Clinton's assessment of contemporary America and her call for a revolutionary paradigm shift can be summarized by repeating over and over again the following mantra: Individualism, selfishness and greed were the virtues of the Reagan '80s. Self-sacrifice, community and altruism will be the virtues of the Clinton '90s.

In the wake of relentless public ridicule over these kinds of statements, Michael Lerner, Mrs. Clinton's principal intellectual guru, leapt to the first lady's defense with a more polished definition of the politics of meaning. "The basic supposition is this," Lerner wrote in the *Wall Street Journal*: "Human beings have psychological, ethical and spiritual needs that transcend the normal liberal agenda. Liberals have tended to focus exclusively on economic entitlements and political rights. But most people need something more: We need to be part of loving families and ethically and spiritually grounded communities that provide a meaning for our lives that transcends the individualism and me-firstism of the competitive market." Lerner is clear in his desire that the politics of meaning transcend "the 'rights'-oriented focus of so much traditional liberal politics."

So what does all this gobbledygook mean in practical terms? How would the politics of meaning be implemented by the Clinton Administration? Lerner recently advised Mrs. Clinton while having dinner at the White House to institute the following policy: "I proposed that the Clinton Administration establish a policy where, for any proposed legislation or new program, there would have to be written first an Ethical and Community Environmental Impact Report, which would require each agency to report how the proposed legislation or new program would impact on shaping ethics and the caring and sharing of the community covered by that agency." Lerner later spelled out in greater detail how the politics of meaning could be translated from theory into practice.

His proposals included: that the Department of Labor order "every workplace" in America "to create a mission statement explaining its function and what conception of the common good it is serving and how it is doing so"; "Honor Labor" campaigns would be sponsored "to highlight the honor due to people for their contributions to the common good," and "a corps of union personnel, worker representatives and psychotherapists" would be trained "in the relevant skills to assist developing a new spirit of cooperation, mutual caring and dedication to work." Lerner, the one-time leader of a revolutionary Marxist organization, is reported to have officiated at his own New Left wedding, which included the bride and groom exchanging rings made out of the fuselage of a U.S. aircraft shot down by the communists over Viet Nam. Born of the 1960s, the politics of meaning represents the political and cultural institutionalization of New Left radicalism.

Although more circumspect in his avowal of the politics of meaning, the president has offered the country his own watered-down version. In his acceptance speech after the November election, president-elect Clinton called for a "New Covenant," one that would redefine the duties of citizens and the responsibilities of the federal government. He said that what is most needed in America is "a new spirit of community, a sense that we're all in this together." The moral basis for this new covenant, said candidate Clinton, is the notion of "reciprocal obligation." His two favorite words in recent speeches have been "sacrifice" and "security." The president's faustian bargain asks the American people to trade a great deal of their freedom in exchange for an economic and moral security that only the President, the first lady, and their corps of social planners can provide. We must give up our selfish interests for the common good and in return the state will take care of all our needs.

But this kind of self-abnegation cuts against the grain of human nature. This is where the first lady and Michael Lerner re-enter. Reinventing government will not be possible until the first lady redefines "who we are as human beings."

One is tempted to ask what will happen to those who are unable or unwilling to see what Mrs. Clinton sees? What of those who will openly resist or fight her reforms? Tipper Gore has a partial answer: She believes that under the Clinton Health Plan *all* Americans should and will have check-ups for mental illness. Does this mean that the angst and sense of meaninglessness that we all feel as a result of having lived through the Reagan years can be ameliorated through nation-wide sessions of collective therapy?

In college, high school and even in elementary school classrooms all across America, there is already a concerted effort underway to indoctrinate our young people in the ideology of '60s radicalism. Traditional education is out and consciousness raising is in. It should not surprise us, then, to learn that the Clinton administration represents a who's who of campus thought police. Donna Shalala (secretary for Health and Human Services) and Sheldon Hackney (chairman of the National Endowment for the Humanities) to name just two, presided over the installation and enforcement of speech codes on their respective campuses during their tenure as university presidents. Verbal morality statutes, "sensitivity" classes and explicitly politicized classes dealing with questions of race, class, gender and sexual orientation now have the unofficial sanction of the Clinton government. Attitude readjustment rather than the reading of great books has become the purpose of these politically correct reeducation camps.

Like any messianic ideology, the politics of meaning thrives on the existence of an easily identifiable enemy. Mrs. Clinton's redefinition of American citizenship begins therefore by exposing those who represent the focus of evil in this post-modern world. A criminal, according to the first lady, is not a man who violates the rights of individuals; he is a man who injures "the common interest." It goes without saying that businessmen are the worst offenders, the new criminals. In a number of public jeremiads, the first lady has named some of America's leading villains: Top on her hit list are the "price gougers," the "cost-shifters" and the "unconscionable profiteers" of the medical-industrial complex, that is, the insurance and drug companies and doctors.

Given Mrs. Clinton's distaste for the free-enterprise system, it is not surprising that two of the president's closest economic advisors have called for an end to America's free-market system. Lester Thurow, an economics professor at M.I.T. has written that "the individualistic Anglo-Saxon British-American form of capitalism" must be replaced in favor of something he calls "communitarian capitalism." Likewise, Robert A. Reich, the president's Secretary of Labor, has argued in his *Tales of a New America* (1987) that America can only be saved by a kind of "collective entrepreneurship."

One is tempted to say that the meaning of the politics of meaning is that it has no meaning. But ideas have consequences, even incoherent ideas, and those notions can be seductive and dangerous, particularly to a culture that has lost its moral compass.

It is now possible to see why the completion of the New Deal is not the end, but rather is the beginning, the launching-off point, the "great leap forward" for St. Hillary's New Salvation. Mrs. Clinton's politics of meaning is but a moral preparation for what is to follow. By clearing the moral atmosphere of traditional American virtues—rationality, independence, self-reliance, frugality, individualism—the politics of meaning hopes to reinvent the American character by establishing the sanctity of self-sacrifice as the highest moral virtue. By delegitimizing the moral foundations for individualism, the way will have been cleared for newer and higher forms of communal action. Once achieved, the American soul will have been opened or prepared for new and ominous forms of social experimentation.

But this kind of moral reformation cannot be achieved without dramatically increasing the coercive powers of the State. And the Clintons have all kinds of bright ideas to reinvent the ways that government can intrude into our private and public lives. Of course the core of the Clinton plan to reconstitute the human soul begins with their Health Care Plan. Make no mistake about it: this is socialist-corporatism pure and simple. If you doubt this, examine the sweeping powers given to the proposed National Health Board. This central committee of seven will function like a Communist Central Committee or one of the Fascist National Councils of Italy. The Clinton's Health Board will oversee and regulate all the activities and operations of the government-created "regional health care alliances," and it will undoubtedly have the authority to enforce wage and price controls. The nation now stands poised on the brink of the largest increase in government controls and government subsidies since the New Deal.

But where exactly does the Founders' Constitution grant the power to the national government to force citizens to participate in a federally-mandated health care plan? To the Clintons and the New Left radicals who support them, such questions are simply irrelevant. The Constitution is at best what the cultural Left says it is and at its worst a retrograde check on the revolutionary goals of the far-Left. If the Clinton's health care plan passes, there will be no limits, no restraints on the leviathan powers of the national government. "Thereafter," writes David B. Rivkin of the *Wall Street Journal*, "Congress will be able to regulate you not because of who you are, what you do for a living, or whether you use the interstate highways, but merely because you exist." But we shouldn't put all the blame on the Clintons: In the end it will have been the American people who drove the final stake into the heart of the Constitution of 1787.

If you want to oppose the politics of meaning and the Clintons' moral-political agenda, you must challenge its basic principles: New Age mysticism, altruism, self-sacrifice, collectivism, elitism, and statism. The politics of freedom must replace the politics of meaning.

A new generation of young people, the new revolutionaries, must rediscover and consistently defend the principles of our Founding Fathers: the idea of individual rights, the sanctity of private property and the inviolability of contract, limited government and the virtues of entrepreneurship. Then and only then will America hold out the promise for a new birth of freedom.

— 10 —

President Clinton's Presidential Rhetoric

Jeffrey J. Poelvoorde

The American people require, and probably want, a president who is willing to lie to them. What they do not need or want is a president who is peculiarly *given* to lying to them. Therein lies the greatest dilemma in Bill Clinton's understanding of presidential leadership, and one that may undo his presidency. In politics, no less than in larger life, it is a great intellectual and moral error to mistake the part for the whole of something. If presidential leadership is a delicate balancing act between truthfulness and lying or concealment, then President Clinton sees only part of the nature of presidential leadership through presidential rhetoric, the part that generates the freedom to govern through secrecy and deception. From the beginning of his campaign for the presidency through his first year of office, President Clinton has demonstrated a too eager willingness to substitute obfuscation—as complexity, vagueness or actual lying—for explanation. If he persists in this tendency, President Clinton may weaken not only his own presidency, but also subsequent ones, too, in addition to inflicting damage upon the already tenuous public trust in our governing institutions.

THE PRESIDENCY AND TRUTHFULNESS

Woodrow Wilson characterized the presidency as "the vital center of action" in the American political system. This comment stands in a tradition of commentary on the American presidency stretching back to Alexander Hamilton's essays in the *Federalist*. There, in *Federalist* No. 70, arguing for the necessity of "unity" in the presidency, Hamilton mentions the "secrecy and despatch" which a single individual will be able to summon in pursuing the peculiar tasks of executive power, in particular, defending the nation and enforcing the laws. Additionally, Hamilton argues, the executive is critical in resisting forces of instability and anarchy which are endemic to democratic government. Continuing this theme through the next several papers, Hamilton presents a presidency which, anticipating Wilson's description, must be able to serve, obey, lead and resist the people, in addition to occasionally acting independently of their wishes.

Out of this complexity in the office of the presidency derives the necessity, or even the centrality, of a kind of presidential rhetoric as a critical component of presidential action. Presidential rhetoric has several functions in terms of presidential governance. Perhaps the main function is to explain the aims, characteristics and demands of the policies towards which a president may wish to lead the nation. Such explanation consists of clarifying the fundamental principles that underlie the policies. Also, it must make the American people aware of the consequences and costs of following those policies. The president owes this kind of explanation so that the American people can play their proper role in participating in the nation's common good and in evaluating the president's performance. Without doubt, this kind of rhetorical responsibility demands truthfulness in the president.

But, even so, the president must occasionally resort to lying or concealment. The necessity for secrecy and deception stems from the harshness of the world and the challenges that it poses to a nation's interest and survival and from the limits of popular understanding of the complexities of governance. Most Americans would probably admit the necessity and probity of the first justification for secrecy and deception; they would tend to call it "national security" or "defense" or even part of the strategy of enforcing the law, say, against organized crime. Seeing the limits of the popular understanding of governance would be more difficult for most of us, though. Yet, as Hamilton reminds us, the president must occasionally resist or ignore the will of the people. Although public opinion is unquestionably the necessary anchor for decent government, its shallowness, transience and partiality cannot provide the sufficient conditions for good government.

The delicacy in presidential leadership is *resorting* to secrecy and deception without *reducing* presidential rhetoric to it. Presidential deception is akin to John Locke's understanding of "executive prerogative" in the *Second Treatise of Government*. Its justification is necessity; it must be used for the public good; and, it must be used sparingly. The alternative is to replace the normal processes of government with the abnormal. And, as Locke suggests with executive prerogative, presidential deception must probably give way to public explanation in most cases. There can be excesses in both directions, too. Not only did Jimmy Carter try to micromanage the complexities of his policies, he probably tried too strenuously to explain everything to the American people. Striving to break down the distinction between presidential reasoning and public reasoning, he wanted to democratize his presidency as much as possible. George Bush may have "underrhetorized" his presidency, so that the American people may eventually have lost sight of what the principles of his adminstration were, to the extent of becoming convinced that perhaps none existed. Richard Nixon may have been relatively forthright in the explanations of his broad policies, but in attempting to contain the damage to his administration unleashed by the Watergate break-in, he appeared to resort so frequently to lying that he eventually lost the trust of the American people.

That delicate balance between truthfulness and deceit is what President Clinton does not appear to understand. Too often in his campaign for, and his conduct of, the presidency, he has resorted to rhetoric that either conceals or distorts the truth. This has taken two characteristic forms: a rhetoric that is so vague and/or complex that it constitutes a form of lying; and apparently deliberate lying. If lying is occasionally permissible and necessary for the president, then what is wrong with President Clinton's version of presidential lying? The main problem, again, is that deceitfulness lies closer to the core of President Clinton's presentation of himself and his program than necessity requires or probity permits.

VAGUENESS AND COMPLEXITY AS LYING

The rhetorical centerpiece of President Clinton's campaign was "Change." It may be that the American public was uneasy about the soundness of the economy and President Bush's ability to fashion or administer suitable policies to address the nation's economic woes. It may also be that the end of the Cold War suggested the necessity of a new set of priorities in American foreign policy. Also, the apparent inability of the Republican adminstration and Democratic Congress to restrain the growth of the federal deficit generated enough disaffection with the status quo to open the door to Ross Perot's serious third-candidate challenge. But aside from several specific criticisms levied against President Bush's administration, the major thrust of what candidate Clinton was offering the country was "change," repeated frequently enough to make the transition from slogan to mantra. Other than giving expression to the prevailing unease or discontent, what did "change" reveal about the probable direction of the country under a potential Clinton administration, or about the content of Democratic ideology which might guide him? The core of Governor Clinton's strategy was to dodge content sufficiently so as to avoid the charge of being too "liberal." Looking at Michael Dukakis's defeat in 1988, Mr. Clinton may have concluded that Americans' discontent with President Bush may not necessarily have signaled a rejection on their part of the ideology that had kept Republicans in the presidency for over a decade and a readiness to embrace an activist Democratic national agenda. "Change" offered something different, but not something discernibly different.

The major initiatives offered by President Clinton since he assumed office—deficit reduction and health care reform— have been shrouded in the same kind of vagueness as his campaign. The thrust of the president's budget plan, aside from some specific taxing proposals that were abandoned during the process of Congressional negotiation, was bland declamation about equal spending cuts and tax increases.

Complexity may distort and conceal as effectively as vagueness. The process of the formation of President Clinton's health care reform proposal (under conditions approximating a national security crisis), let alone its content, suggest an attempt to fashion policy so complex that it defies explanation and resists criticism. True, President Clinton has stated what appears to be a broad principle underlying his proposal (universal coverage with no real increase in federal spending). The plan is so multifarious, however, that it is almost impossible for the public to see it as an embodiment of that simple principle. One could say in defense of the president that his plan is complex because the issue is complex, and that no other available simpler option (such as Canada's "single-payer plan") avoids insurmountable objections. But one could just as easily argue that the plan's complexity stems from the necessity of concealing the genuine scope of the changes proposed, their costs and their consequences for the public.

LYING AS LYING

Governor Clinton campaigning for the presidency repeatedly called for a "middle-class tax cut." President Clinton hastily abandoned the idea. Vice-President Bush campaigning in 1988 promised no new taxes. President Bush in 1990 signed one of the largest tax increases in United States history. Is there a difference? In the extent that there is a difference between changing one's mind and lying, then there is a difference between these two "discrepancies" between campaigning and governing. The rationale for President Clinton abandoning a major aspect of his proposed plan for middle-class tax relief was that he did not know until he occupied the presidency how serious the deficit would be. If he had not repeatedly during the campaign, however, declaimed on the seriousness of the deficit, occasionally estimating its potential growth far in excess of what became the basis of his budget plan, one would be inclined to accept this rationale more seriously. Admittedly, moralizing about the "inaccuracies" uttered in the course of campaigning may seem a little precious, since this appears to be intrinsic to campaigning in America. But there is a difference between prudential shifts in policy, even occasionally exaggerated campaign polemics, and an extensive ruse to offset fears of tax increases. During his tenure in office, President Clinton has repeatedly demonstrated the same willingness to resort to deceit for policy purposes. Concealing tax increases as spending cuts (Medicare cost shifting), scapegoating pharmaceutical companies for rising medical costs, or obscuring the number of Americans who are likely to pay higher costs for health care, all suggest a pattern of indifference to truth which far outweighs the importance of, say, concealing the truth about extra-marital affairs.

THE POTENTIAL EFFECTS OF
PRESIDENT CLINTON'S RHETORIC

If this characterization of President Clinton's rhetorical tendencies is correct, what explains it? Character may be part of it, although one should be slow to accuse anyone of endemic hypocrisy. The apparent evasions, inconsistencies and obscurities in President Clinton's public demeanor may derive from simple confusion stemming from embracing too many different kinds of policies, or as with health care reform, attempting to put together a package of reforms that tries to address as many potential criticisms as possible. Perhaps

President Clinton does not believe in the rhetorical component of policy-making or the necessity of public explanation. More likely, President Clinton is caught between two sets of tensions generated by two different groups: Democrats and the American people. In order to maintain his governing base within the Democratic party, President Clinton must negotiate between the more activist or "progressive" wing of his party and its moderate center, of which he has presented himself as something of a spokesman. Although both of these groups wear the label "Democrat," they have somewhat different policy aims and views of the proper scope and activity of the national government. Trying to hold together contending factions in his party may incline him to verbal appeasement or vague rationalizations (and policies). When he has been most straightforward in advocating a policy, as with NAFTA, he has openly embraced the alienation of major components of his Democratic coalition.

The other group with whom President Clinton must deal is the American people. He probably senses the ambivalence that many—perhaps most—Americans feel towards many of his initiatives, even the initiatives of a centrist Democrat. Attempting to give vent to their worries, while not closing off his political flexibility by actually suggesting a clear policy to overcome the conditions that may be generating the worries, he has resorted (as we saw above) to vague bromides such as "change" that say everything and nothing at the same time.

If he persists in this emergent pattern, his ability to summon public support—translating into Congressional support—may dwindle, rendering his presidency increasingly impotent. One can resort too frequently and too trustingly to the "oracle" of presidential "approval ratings," but they are a barometer of some elusive quality of public confidence in the trustability, if not the competence, of the president. The outlook at the end of President Clinton's first year is not encouraging. Too, the acid effects of cheapened presidential rhetoric by President Clinton may extend into subsequent administrations. Might the presidency as the "vital center of action" be rendered less powerful, less capable to deal with the exigencies of the nation because an enduring sense of distrust will have crept into the public's view of the office? Last, the already significant sense of alienation on the part of many Americans (the nearly twenty percent of the electorate that voted for Ross Perot in 1992?) from the public institutions of American political life may be intensified if President Clinton continues to resort to presidential rhetoric as a cloaking device for his policies.

What should he do? First, it is important to recollect that President Clinton possesses considerable political skills, in the best sense of the word. The capacity to negotiate and compromise with opponents, native intelligence, and an ability to construct coalitions over contentious issues—all of these are valuable talents. He could use these talents to offer simpler and clearer policies, genuinely intended, with clearer and more straightforward rationales attached. Also, he could offer actual *policies*, rather than general policy dispositions. As mentioned, an example of the latter is his budget package, in reality worked out between Congressional leaders, supposedly under the rubric of a few presidential principles tossed in by Mr. Clinton. Yet, as mentioned above, he appeared to offer real leadership in prosecuting the cause of NAFTA—a real policy, controversial as it was. The president appeared capable of summoning real arguments and engaging in substantive debate. Now, in order to do this, he may have to relinquish attempting to appease all and sundry factions in his party—as he was willing to do with NAFTA—and forge a governing coalition with his partisan opponents. But, at least in doing so, he appeared to be a forceful leader arguing passionately and compellingly—and honestly—for a distinct policy. He may have generated some political enemies and lost some of his traditional Democratic support. But what he gained in the apprehension of the general public may probably outweigh those losses.

CONCLUSION

Charity demands that we be patient with learners. We do not know, only one year into President Clinton's presidency, whether, and how much of, his missteps may be attributable to amateurism or what may derive from character defects or even from a defective view of his office. Therefore, he deserves a certain amount of indulgence before final judgment. Too, his prior record in office suggests the ability to overcome his defects. It is, however, dangerous to generalize from prior experience, simply because the demands of the presidency are different in kind from the challenges that Clinton has previously faced. Perhaps boyish charm laced with Rhodes-scholar intellectualism and rural Southernisms was sufficient to negotiate his personal and political collisions with the truth while Bill Clinton was governor of Arkansas, and even to propel him over media and voter scrutiny during the arduous but jaunty process of campaigning for the presidency. But we want more prudence—more *capacity*—when a man is occupying the greatest office leading the greatest people of the greatest contemporary nation.

Aristotle teaches us to search for the virtuous mean between the vicious extremes. Somewhere between Jimmy Carter's democratic earnestness and Bill Clinton's democratic deceptiveness lies prudent republican leadership. If Bill Clinton refuses to learn that lesson, he may indeed discover the American people's likely preference for a Republican mean between two Democratic extremes.

— 11 —

The Unraveling of
the Clinton Presidency

Patrick B. McGuigan

The majority of political personalities present through their words and their works sufficient nuances, complexities and contradictions to defy facile categorization. Consequently, care must be taken to avoid sweeping generalities. This is not the case with William Jefferson Clinton, for the specifics support the generalities. An impressive campaigner, Clinton is a horrible president. After a year, his record has few redeeming aspects, and the future looks certain to bring more of the same.

CLINTON, GERGEN AND TRUTH:
INEVITABLE CONFLICT?

Many contemporary broadcast and print commentators regard politics as an elaborate game. Such pundits gave high marks to the former Arkansas governor, a Democrat, when he turned to Republican David Gergen early in his presidency.

The generally liberal press hailed Clinton's astuteness in choosing the GOP political mechanic. Many conservatives reacted with fury at what they perceived as Gergen's betrayal in accepting the president's call to service.

A dissenter among the conservatives was Paul Weyrich, for whom I worked throughout the 1980s. Weyrich accurately predicted that Gergen would help Clinton rebuild credibility, writing that "amidst the pygmies in the Clinton White House" Gergen "is truly a giant. Some have called him a traitor for taking the job. In fact, his views have been consistent since the Reagan administration. He is a raging moderate." Weyrich called Gergen's selection "both brilliant and dangerous. . . . (B)rilliant because Gergen is someone who, if Clinton follows his advice, can shape up the Clinton presidency. . . . It is dangerous . . . because I believe (Clinton) lies as a matter of course. . . . Now all presidents lie and Gergen has . . . seen his share of presidential fibbing up close. But Clinton is a big time liar, so much so I doubt he even knows when he is telling the truth. . . . (W)hen (Gergen) is asked to lie himself on a matter of significance, I believe he has enough integrity to resign." Whether or not his judgement proves correct about David Gergen, after one year there remains no doubt that Weyrich's assessment of Clinton is on the mark.

CLINTON TAKES CHARGE:
MENDACITY IN THE OVAL OFFICE

President Clinton has audacious disregard for truth, and for his own past rhetoric. In July 1993, in a speech at Fort McNair, President Clinton claimed the first time he had ever considered the military's policy on homosexuals was after an October 1991 Harvard speech: "I was asked by one of the students what I thought of . . . lifting the ban. This question had never been presented to me and I never had the opportunity to discuss it with anyone."

A newspaper called *Bay Windows* in September 1991 reported "Clinton . . . told reporters and a key member of Congress that he opposes the Pentagon's ban on gay and lesbian service personnel." Clinton belittled the military's policy in an early 1992 Associated Press interview. Later, in a speech to Hollywood activists, he denigrated it as "quaint little rules."

Politicians often dissemble, fudge or change their minds. (A notable pre-Clinton example of this was George Bush's disastrous switch of his 1988 "no new taxes" pledge.) But Bill Clinton is in a class by himself. Leaving aside the private affairs and his military record, there is enough evidence on public issues to merit taking everything he says with a grain of salt.

Candidate Clinton decried the deficit, promising "a choice between a children's tax credit or a significant reduction in ... income tax rate" for the middle class. As president he changed: "We just have to face the fact that to make the changes our country needs, more Americans must contribute today."

Candidate Clinton promised to slice the deficit to zero, though at times the promise was to trim it by half. But President Clinton signed an economic plan that will, under the most optimistic scenarios, cut the deficit by only 11 percent.

President Clinton had a unique opportunity to tackle entitlements and other spending programs which drain economic vitality. Instead, he raised taxes on workers and employers, violating promises he made to watch out for the middle class. As details of his tax plan emerged in the spring of 1993, opposition solidified.

Candidate Clinton opposed federal excise gas tax hikes, but President Clinton lobbied aggressively for increases. Americans of $20,000-plus annual income—truck drivers, for example—discovered that in Bill Clinton's America, they are "the rich."

Candidate Clinton favored a line-item veto, but as president settled for "enhanced recision authority." (U.S. Rep. Ernest Istook, R-Oklahoma City, called it "line-item voodoo.")

Candidate Clinton denounced the Reagan-Bush years, alleging in May 1992 that America had "continued to lose ground in overall productivity growth." Candidate Clinton told manufacturers the U.S. had fallen behind in "infrastructure investment, in . . . communications and transportation" and on and on. President Clinton (October 20, 1993) saw things differently: "In the last 12 or 13 years, we have seen productivity in the United States go up at 4 percent or more a year. . . . We've had two European companies put plants in North America. They could have gone to Mexico. Where did they go? They went to South Carolina. One is now going to Alabama. Why? Because it's cheaper. Because labor is highly productive, even though it's more expensive."

Candidate Clinton backed budget cuts for Congress itself, but President-elect Clinton backed off. Candidate Clinton promised to "hit the ground running" with a vigorous first 100 days, while President Clinton's first 100 days were stunning for ineptitude and lethargy.

Bill Clinton is the man who, in a speech to black pastors in November 1993, spoke eloquently of America's "great crisis of the spirit." Indeed.

BILL CLINTON'S AMERICA

By the end of 1993, President Clinton figured out how to move legislation through Congress. On the North American Free Trade Agreement, he bought the votes needed for victory with the most breath-taking use of pork-barrel since Lyndon Johnson.

As distressing as is his economic agenda, it is in the cultural and legal arenas that Clinton crosses the line into radicalism.

The president targeted the Second Amendment rights of law-abiding citizens. He promoted legislation which will make even peaceful pro-life demonstrators criminals under federal law.

We can expect worse. Clinton entered office opposing any restrictions on abortion (as a state politician, he backed moderate curbs). He endorsed the lethal logic of *Roe* v. *Wade*, pushed taxpayer abortion funding and announced a judicial litmus test. He backed laws which would assure the destruction of even more unborn children.

Landmark Legal Foundation, a public interest law center based in Kansas City, Missouri, concluded in spring 1993: "Not in decades has politics driven the U.S. Department of Justice (DOJ) as it has in the Clinton Administration's first 100 days. . . . (Attorney General) Janet Reno's first act, . . . firing of all U.S. Attorneys, signaled the administration's primary objective to clear the ranks of previous administrations regardless of the consequences for the American people."

Landmark president Jerald L. Hill proved prophetic. As this presidency advanced, Attorney General Reno and President Clinton concentrated on defending homosexuals in the military (and then invited challenges to the "don't ask, don't tell" compromise) and Hillary Rodham Clinton's closed door health care meetings, rather than on traditional law enforcement efforts. Clinton's anti-crime agenda consisted of spending a lot of money on programs of dubious merit while taking guns away from the law-abiding.

Landmark's "100 Days of Disappointment" warned of the Department's "overly political nature" as the agency went "out of control." The group understated its case, given Clinton-Reno briefs through late 1992, on everything from homosexuality to child pornography (where Clinton eventually reversed Reno after public and congressional outcry).

One astonishing choice for a top DOJ post was University of Pennsylvania law professor Lani Guinier. A bit of historical revisionism has followed Guinier's weeks in the Washington meat-grinder, so a review of the facts is in order.

The president's nominee to run the Civil Rights Division was, as Clint Bolick of the Institute for Justice observed, "breathtakingly radical." In law review articles, she attacked American governance, dismissing democratic rule as "permanent majority hegemony." She supported "proportionate interest representation for self-identified communities of interest." Her rejection of coalitions repudiated civil rights tradition.

Guinier's complicated vision was summarized by columnist John Leo as granting "a minority veto over some majority decisions, and she talks of using the Voting Rights Act to ensure equal prospects of political satisfaction. Disadvantaged minorities should have 'a voice that dependably produces policy satisfaction through the political process.'" Who defines "political" or "policy" satisfaction? Guinier: "Fringe groups with illegitimate preferences would be represented, but if their preferences prevailed, the resulting legislation would be vulnerable under existing constitutional analysis."

Her nomination was eventually withdrawn by a president who said he never read her writings, yet Clinton and Reno brought to the highest echelons of government dozens of lawyers just as far outside the mainstream of traditional culture and law.

Clinton, Reno and Senate Judiciary Committee Chairman Joseph Biden, D-Delaware, were stunned at opposition to former Duke University law professor Walter Dellinger III, who on October 13 gained 65-34 Senate confirmation to another high post at DOJ. Concerns about Dellinger's temperament, however, continued. Dellinger wrote some of Biden's floor speeches during the debate over Robert Bork's 1987 nomination to the Supreme Court. Jesse Helms and other Republicans criticized the liberal law professor's relentless political activism. Dellinger refused to offer specifics about his role in the anti-Bork coalition, leading conservatives to support a Helms filibuster. Helms finally gave up, but not before making it clear that he and some colleagues would apply to liberals the same rules applied to conservative nominees 1981-92. That determination came not a moment too soon.

Another nominee will reach the Senate about the time this book is released in early 1994. The record of Rosemary Barkett of Florida's Supreme Court conflicts with the "tough on crime" image Clinton and Reno tried to fashion for themselves. Barkett categorized one murder as "not simply a homicide case" but "also a social awareness case. Wrongly, but rightly in the eyes of (the murderer), this killing was effectuated to focus attention on a chronic and pervasive illness of racial discrimination and of hurt, sorrow and rejection." Barkett was Clinton's choice for the Eleventh U.S. Circuit Court of Appeals, covering Florida, Georgia and Alabama.

In November 1993, as he and Reno presented themselves as determined foes of crime, Clinton's choice for the Sixth U.S. Court of Appeals neared Senate approval. As Marianne Lombardi of the conservative Free Congress Foundation said, Martha Craig Daughtrey, then an associate justice for Tennessee, has a record "in stark contrast to Clinton's rhetoric. . . . Clinton may talk right but he governs left. . . . (T)he nominees he is choosing for lifetime appointments to the federal bench say much more about him than his scripted soundbites."

As for lifetime appointments, there was no solace in Clinton's first Supreme Court justice. Ruth Bader Ginsburg is a nice person with an agenda. On the High Court, she will continue the erosion of democratic governance, replacing it with judicial oligarchy. That she will do this with "sensitivity" provides little comfort to those who hoped Clinton might find a person to follow the example of Byron White, the generally principled jurist she replaced. Ginsburg is a White-style moderate in some areas of economics. But, as conservative Tom Jipping put it, "In key categories of cases e.g., cases involving the separation of powers, abortion, standing or discrimination, her politics drives her jurisprudence."

Before the Senate Judiciary Committee, Ginsburg refused to answer questions about explicit constitutional provisions, including the Second Amendment's protection of the right to keep and bear arms, and the death penalty. And yet she embraced philosophies found nowhere in the Constitution or its amendments. She was comfortable with the precedent in *Roe* v. *Wade*. She sympathized with "gay rights," leaving informed readers to conclude she will embrace assertions of a constitutional right to homosexual activity.

On contentious social issues, Ginsburg comes down politely on the side of Harvard University Professor Larry Tribe's view of law: In modern America, the liberal agenda is constitutionally required, whereas the conservative agenda is constitutionally forbidden. It is easy to oppose Larry Tribe. It is harder to oppose a person of Ginsburg's charm, personality and obvious ability. Yet, her philosophy will take her further and further into the realm of anti-democratic activism. A nice lady, yes, but as Jipping observed, "If Judge Ginsburg is in the mainstream, she is at its left bank."

A key player in Clinton's Department of Justice drama is Webster Hubbell, a former law partner of Hillary who took over as associate attorney general. Hubbell was a long-time member of the Country Club of Little Rock, which Governor Clinton used to frequent. In March 1992, civil rights leaders denounced Clinton for "betrayal" after he golfed at the club, which had no black members. Clinton apologized, and said he would not return to the club until it was integrated. Hubbell remained a member, and that became an issue during his confirmation proceedings. As Coalitions for America, the conservative lobbying organization, asserted: "(T)he perversion of the confirmation process brought about by Democrats since 1987 will never be addressed until they are forced to live by the rules they created." Hubbell's membership was the focus of stories in *The New York Times*, *Washington Times*, *Arkansas Democrat-Gazette* and *Washington Post*. He withdrew from the club and gained confirmation.

But the tale does not end there. The powerful Rose law firm of Little Rock, of which he and the president's wife are alumni, had represented Madison Guaranty, a savings and loan owned by close allies from Clinton's Arkansas years. Hubbell sued auditors on behalf of the S&L. Vince Foster, the White

House aide who killed himself in summer 1993, had also represented a leading figure in the Madison S&L scandal. One person implicated in the scandal fingered both the president and his successor as governor, Jim Guy Tucker, for pressuring the S&L into suspect loans. In early winter 1993, Hubbell and the U.S. Attorney for Little Rock recused themselves from a Department of Justice investigation as it drew closer to Clinton. Attorney General Janet Reno ignored calls for appointment of an independent counsel, even as controversy touched the president, his wife, and much of the top leadership at the department. Welcome to Bill Clinton's America.

CLINTON ABROAD: DRIFT, DENIAL AND LOOMING DISASTER

Lack of prior foreign policy experience is not necessarily debilitating to a presidency. Building on the legacy of his predecessors, Bill Clinton enjoyed some successes forging a good relationship with Russian President Boris Yeltsin and supporting the tenuous peace framework for Israel and the Palestine Liberation Organization. Some who are adept—Ronald Reagan is one example—had no formal foreign policy experience before their presidencies. However, successful presidents have shared a belief that American policy should secure American interests. A rational framework guided their decisions on use of force and diplomacy.

Clinton has few core principles and no apparent framework—other than, perhaps, a predilection to trust internationalists more than American military leaders. As a result, he lurches from one crisis to the next. His on-the-job training is exacting a high price in U.S. prestige and influence. When commentators noted U.S. foreign policy "drift" in late

1993, a better word might have been "aimlessness." Bill Clinton never brought moral persuasion, let alone rational deployment of force, effectively to bear on the most horrifying world spectacle of 1993—the final devastation of what used to be called Yugoslavia.

Yet even in areas where American strength might have effectively been used to advance American interests, Clinton proved inept. After hundreds of thousands of Haitian refugees, given a green light, fled to America in dangerous boats, he reversed course and embraced policies he had denounced throughout 1992. As events in Haiti reeled out of control, military leaders (whom State Department aide Lawrence E. Pezzullo had dubbed "chicken littles") proved as prophetic about "nation building" in that Caribbean island nation as in Somalia. Clinton ignored military advisors, sending a lightly-armed contingent of U.S. "civic assistance" troops. When their ship tried to dock in Port-au-Prince, angry demonstrators prevented unloading. *The Washington Post* commented in an editorial (October 14, 1993): "The abrupt collapse of U.S. plans to land soldiers in Haiti has dealt a new blow to President Clinton's attempts to demonstrate that he has a coherent foreign policy capable of leading the world community toward a post-Cold War era of diplomacy and stability."

Clinton's handling of military involvement in Somalia is the best-known example of his international failures. Whether for cynical or other reasons, Clinton in late 1992 endorsed his predecessor's "clearly-defined humanitarian mission.... The mandate our armed forces and our partners in the coalition will fulfill is to create a secure environment to save lives and I commended President Bush for his leadership on this important humanitarian effort." That mission was accomplished by summer 1993. But Clinton switched to an ill-defined course of nation-building. U.S. commanders grew perplexed about "mission creep", an expansion of responsibilities without increased resources. Former President Bush graciously declined to second guess our confusion on the world stage. Only once did Bush confess he worried "about the mission having been redefined. Our mission was to go into Somalia, open the supply lines (and) then to withdraw and have the United Nations handle the peacekeeping function."

Aimlessness can yield disaster. Defense Secretary Les Aspin, in a fateful decision in early fall, denied a military request for vehicles with reinforced hulls. That proved literally fatal when an American Ranger unit suffered 70 percent casualties in Mogadishu. The losses were the highest unit casualty rate since the 1965 Ia Drang Valley battle in Vietnam.

At the core of Clinton's Somalian failure was his apparent belief that the U.S. military should become an arm of U.N. Secretary General Boutros Boutros-Ghali's international vision. Former Defense Secretary Dick Cheney, on former President Bush's behalf, had consistently "resisted . . . pleas from the United Nations and others to broaden the mission." But things had changed by fall 1993. In an exchange with Secretary of State Warren Christopher, Boutros-Ghali spoke of his determination "to bring . . . to justice" a Somali warlord. Senator Frank Lautenberg of New Jersey, echoing other Democrats, regarded Clinton's expansion of the mission as "far beyond that . . . originally carved out and understood." Boutros-Ghali's determination, well removed from American interests, led to the death of 17 American soldiers and the wounding of 77 others. In character, Clinton blamed others. *The Washington Post* quoted the president on the transformation of the U.S. military's role in Somalia: "Why didn't I know this was happening?" By year's end, plans were being made for withdrawal from the region.

The world's superpower allowed a U.N. lightweight and a Somali warlord to determine American policy at the Horn of Africa. Amos Perlmutter, writing in *The Washington Post* (October 18, 1993), captured the spectacle: "President Clinton's record in foreign policy is abysmal and shows no sign of improving. It can be characterized by reluctance, reaction, by passivity and false bluster and failure to formulate and articulate a foreign policy."

Clinton ended his first year adrift in foreign affairs, reeling from one misjudgment to another—mistakes leading not to the groves of Oxford philosophers, but to the graves of American soldiers. George Bush knew foreign policy, Bill Clinton does not, and it shows. Regardless of the former president's faults, George Bush's strengths on the world stage make all the more glaring the disastrous failures of his successor.

CONCLUSION: THE LIES WILL CATCH UP

Political handlers masterfully packaged Bill Clinton as the man from Hope, a place where small town values still prevail. Desperate for change after the lethargy of the Bush years, Americans never grasped the truth about Bill Clinton's life: That his formative years were not spent in the nice little town of Hope, but in Hot Springs, the most "wide open" town in the state, and perhaps in the region.

David Broder of *The Washington Post* once charitably mused on Clinton's "trust deficit." This president's politics, character, and consistent distortions—whether the issue is personal shortcomings or public policy—none of this is surprising when the entire story is known. Little wonder that the most persistent, vigorous Clinton critic is the editorial page editor in Little Rock, Paul Greenberg.

Broder's colleague at the *Post*, Robert Samuelson, has expressed with some apparent regret and dismay the insight that Bill Clinton is the biggest liar ever to serve in the presidency. As more and more Americans reach the same conclusion, the Clinton presidency will unravel due not only to its misguided world view, but also to the character flaws of its principal players.

— 12 —

Federal Deficits, Federal Debt, and the Clinton Administration

Mark A. Nadler

Any economist allotted limited space to address the economic policies of the Clinton administration immediately faces the problem of deciding how to allocate this resource to such competing ends as rising health care costs, the poor quality of American education, America's low rate of business investment, the design of optimal environmental policies, NAFTA, controlling federal budget deficits and debt, stimulating economic growth, improving government efficiency, fixing our decrepit welfare system, creating more and better quality jobs, reforming our legal system, repairing our crumbling public infrastructure, reducing government regulation, boosting private savings, etc.

Out of these choices, federal deficits and debt stand out for special consideration for two reasons. First, among all public policy debates, none has been more blurred by misinformation than the issue of federal deficits and debt. Second, among the American electorate, only unemployment is viewed as a more serious problem.

In 1983, I was part of a local public radio panel that was debating federal budgetary deficits and debt. At that time, I argued that given the existing economic theories concerning the impact of budgetary deficits and debt on the real economy, and given the existing empirical evidence, it was impossible for an educated citizen to reach any firm conclusion concerning what actions the federal government should take either in controlling the size of the deficit or debt, or in cutting back federal expenditures, or in substituting taxes for debt.

Hopefully, it's not stubbornness on my part that forces me to come to a similar conclusion today. What I would like to do is to make clear my reasoning in reaching this judgment, and attempt to relate my analysis to President Clinton's 1993 budget.

Tales from the Dark Side

In thinking about the dangerousness of both the size and recent trends of both federal debt and deficits a multitude of viewpoints scream out at us. There are those who, simply, recite the mantra dealing with the sheer dollar size of the federal deficit and debt: "In 1992 the federal deficit was $399,733,000,000 while the federal debt was $4,077,510,000,000." This statement is normally followed by a widening of the eyes by listeners and an "Oh my gosh!". Both the suppliers and demanders of these facts I call "Absolutists" because their belief in the significance of absolute numbers is absolute.

Slightly up the rung in the economic evolutionary ladder are those natives known as the "Relativists." This species repeats without taking a breath between sentences: "Did you know that in 1991 the federal debt was approximately 70 percent of GNP, and in 1992 interest payments consumed 13.5 percent of the federal budget." Like the "Absolutists," "Relativists" believe that the sheer size of something, in this case a relative magnitude, conveys useful information.

Off the same branch as the "Absolutists" and the "Relativists" are "Extrapolists." "Extrapolists" love to predict some coming doom based on their forecasts of current debt and deficit trends which, through the mumbo jumbo of economic modeling, indicates America's forthcoming bankruptcy. Like those religious leaders who make their living predicting the Second Coming, "Extrapolists" claim it might happen next week, next year, next five years, next ten years, and so forth.

Of a completely different genus are "Inflationists" and "Intergenerationalists." "Inflationists" argue that deficits and debt cause inflation while "Intergenerationalists" emphasize the burden debt imposes on future generations of citizens.

On top of this taxonomic pyramid sits many economists and politicians with the one tale that sends shivers down everyone's back: federal government deficits and debt hurt the economy by crowding-out private investment. Normally, the following story is told (mostly in bars and restaurants and not around campfires) in support of this view. When the federal government runs a deficit it must turn toward its financial agent, the Treasury Department, to finance it. The Treasury Department, like any other borrower, must enter private financial markets and try to convince lenders to buy its bills, notes, and bonds it issues to finance the federal government's deficit. One method that Treasury uses to compete against private borrowers is to offer higher interest rates on its debt. This strategy boosts the cost of borrowing money for everyone. Since business borrows to finance capital investments, anything that makes it more expensive to borrow ends up discouraging business investment. When business invests less, workers in the future have less capital to work with which slows gains in labor productivity and the rate at which wages can increase. Now here is one scary story that both mainstream parties in America believe.

WHERE THERE IS DARKNESS THERE IS ALSO LIGHT

Let me address each of these arguments in turn. Citing absolute amounts of money owed, whether talking about a public or private entity, means absolutely nothing. If I tell you that XYZ corporation owes 2 billion dollars, and I ask if this is a large sum to owe, your response should be "insufficient information." If XYZ corporation is a "MOM and POP" business, then it is a large amount to owe. If XYZ corporation is some global behemoth, with hundreds of billions of dollars in world sales, it might not be a lot to owe.

Given what I just said, you might be led to believe that "Relativist" arguments are closer to the truth. Well, yes and no. Relative magnitudes, in general, contain more information than absolute numbers. The trouble with relative numbers is that in making historical comparisons, all kinds of different conclusions can be drawn. For example, in 1792 federal outlays for interest payments were over 50 percent of the federal budget (I bet you did not know that!). Does this mean that the 1992 number for this same statistic at 13.5 percent is small? And in 1945 federal debt was 122.5 percent of GNP. Does this mean that the current ratio of 70 percent is small? All one can answer to these questions is that it depends on historical circumstances.

What about the crashing trend lines produced by "Extrapolists"? Trend analysis suffers from its own set of problems. Human history is full of dire predictions based on extrapolating trends which were wrong—remember the Club of Rome forecasts? A good illustration of how trend line analysis can go awry is a prediction I made a short time ago concerning my daughter Esther. One morning, I found her scratching a small section of her left cheek. Based on the rate she was scratching, I forecast that in 14 months she would reach her right cheek. My wife and I were in a panic. I searched furiously through the yellow pages under the heading *Child Psychologists*. Guess what happened? Yes, you're right! Esther stopped scratching even before I could dial 1-800-281-Freud. My forecast was wrong. Long before she reached the other side of her face, either her itch disappeared or the blood from penetrating her skin stopped her from proceeding. These same sort of events seem to operate over and over again in human history. This is not to say that trends are worthless. It's just that one must be exceedingly careful in drawing conclusions from them, including the one about the "sky falling down" because of upward trends in a set of federal budgetary numbers.

If we define inflation as a continuous rise in the price level over time, then there is absolutely no empirical support linking inflation with federal deficits and debt. Across nations over time, the single most important variable in explaining inflation is excessive printing of money. During the 1980s, when the U.S. deficit and debt skyrocketed, inflation fell dramatically as the Federal Reserve bank regained control over the U.S. money supply.

My personal fondness for "Intergenerationalists" is based on a T.V. commercial they ran a number of years ago illustrating their argument. See if you recognize this scene. The commercial opens with a screaming baby all alone in a crib.

Then a voice (from heaven?) informs us that this child owes $X@#$%*+ dollars on the federal debt, and wouldn't you be screaming if you owed this much? The commercial is intended to get you to give your best "Well, gee, gosh, I guess so."

The problem of screaming babies is easily resolved given the following two facts: first, what the T.V. commercial did not show you were all of those spoiled little smiling brats, who through inheritance, will receive part of the monies owed by the commercial's crybabies; second, while future generations inherit debt from today's generation, they also inherit federally financed goods like bridges, roads, national security, new knowledge supported by federal research grants, etc. Many of these are paid for with federal debt.

Crowding-out is a bit more difficult to address. Nonetheless, two arguments exist which at least put into question the crowding-out story. First, there is an alternative theory, attributable to David Ricardo, on how government borrowing impacts on the economy. The modern version of this view goes by the name Ricardian equivalence. In this view of reality, citizens view government debt as equivalent to government taxes. When the government wants to borrow, citizens recognize that this borrowing will in the future manifest itself as additional taxes which will have a present value equivalent to what is being borrowed today. In response to their predicted increased future tax burden, individuals increase their savings dollar for dollar with increases in government borrowing. The net effect of this is that government borrowing has no effect on interest rates. In addition, under Ricardian equivalence, borrowing and taxes have equivalent effects on the economy. What matters in this world is not how government finances itself, but the size of government. Bigger government means a smaller private sector, and a smaller government means a bigger private sector. If Americans want a larger and more robust private sector, the way to accomplish it is not by substituting taxes for borrowing, but by shrinking the size of the public sector.

Interestingly, there is some empirical evidence to back up this story, which is my second argument against the crowding-out approach. When economists try to measure the relationship between interest rates and government borrowing they either come up with no relationship, a weak positive relationship, or a weak negative relationship. This evidence can be viewed as supporting Ricardian equivalence and undermining crowding-out. Under the crowding-out approach, if interest rates don't rise then business investment won't fall. Unfortunately, part of the empirical evidence also goes against Ricardian equivalence, since private savings seem not to rise by the same magnitude as increases in government deficits. What does all of this mean? Am I saying that deficits and debt in the U.S. are not problems? At the least, theory and evidence suggest that any view we hold on this topic should be tempered with a question mark.

WHEN TO SPEND, WHEN TO TAX, AND WHEN TO BORROW?

Given the ambiguous results on how federal deficits and debt impact on the economy, a tempting alternative strategy, based on public finance, is to study when the federal government should spend, tax, and borrow. This was the strategy President Reagan's advisors tried to present once they realized the extent of the federal deficits that were going to be incurred during his presidency. Unfortunately, their arguments had a disingenuous ring given their previous rhetoric concerning the evils of public indebtedness.

Nevertheless, from a public finance viewpoint I believe they were correct in what they were trying to say. What follows deals with the microeconomics of government spending, taxation, and borrowing.

When to Spend?

Outside of the activities in support of a minimalist state, public finance argues that federal government expenditures should go either to offset various forms of market failure which reduce economic efficiency, or in support of income redistribution. Market failure includes public goods, externalities, imperfect competition, business cycles, and problems related to missing markets. Some common examples of each, stated in operational terms, are national defense (public good), anti-pollution laws (externality), Federal Trade Commission (imperfect competition), fiscal policy (business cycle) and federal flood insurance (missing market).

While market failure or redistribution constitutes a necessary condition for the existence of the federal government, neither of them constitute a sufficient condition. For example, let's say because of the existence of imperfect competition in the computer industry society suffers a loss of $100. It wouldn't make sense for government to spend $200 to fix this problem. More generally, the benefit(s) flowing from the federal government's use of resources should be compared to the benefit(s) those same resources would have produced in the private economy. Only federal government expenditures that can pass this type of benefit/cost test should be made. This sort of reasoning also applies to redistribution expenditures.

When to Tax and When to Borrow?

As important in knowing when the federal government should spend is to know when the federal government should tax and borrow. An important principle in public finance that gives us some guidance on this question is the benefits-principle. As a normative principle, the benefits-principle argues that citizens should pay, through taxes, for the benefits they receive from federal government expenditures. This principle also implies that the federal government, at least partially, finance itself through debt. To illustrate, when a nation engages in a (just) war, the benefits from this conflict accrue to many generations over time. According to the benefits-principle, each of these generations should pay for part of this conflict. The way to accomplish this is to tax and borrow from the generation which is alive during the war, and pay these debts back with taxes paid by future generations.

The benefits-principle also has some implications for economic efficiency. Assume that the federal government is contemplating the construction of a long-lived asset (e.g., roads). If the government's only financing tool was taxation, the generation of citizens alive today might vote against the construction of this asset—even if it could pass a benefits/cost test—based on benefits received today versus costs paid today. Yet these same citizens might be willing to engage in a project that has both current and future benefits and only current costs if future generations of beneficiaries of this asset could be forced to pay part of its bill. The only way this can be accomplished is through government borrowing.

Another reason for federal government borrowing is to achieve intergenerational equity. For better or worse, we have become a society that thinks it's reasonable for the federal government to take from those who have and to give to those who don't. It's simple enough, and even logical, to extend this reasoning to intergenerational transfers. The normal expectation is that future generations of Americans will, on average, be better off than the current generation. If that's true, why not remove wealth from richer future generations and give it to those who are alive today? One way of achieving this is for the government to finance its current consumption with borrowed monies that will be paid back by future generations.

A more subtle argument in support of federal government borrowing involves minimizing, what economists call, excess burden. Excess burden is the difference between the dollar pain associated with a tax and the dollar taxes actually paid. Take the example of the $100 I pay in federal income taxes every year. If the actual dollar pain of this tax equals $120 then my excess burden is $20. At least in theory, excess burden is exponentially related to tax rates. That is, if you double a tax rate, excess burden more than doubles. Under these circumstances, if government experiences the need to increase its spending, it might make sense to finance this increase both through borrowing and a small tax rate increase spread over time. This financing package would impose fewer excess burdens on taxpayers than one which increased taxes sufficiently to pay for the whole spending increase at once.

A PUBLIC FINANCE ANALYSIS OF PRESIDENT CLINTON'S 1993 BUDGET PLAN

Given what I just argued, it's irrelevant that President Clinton's 1993 budget is called a deficit reduction package.

It's also irrelevant what impact his budget will have on future deficits and debt. From a public finance perspective, what matters for any public budget, is its impact on improving economic efficiency—by correcting for various forms of market failure—and income distribution. Applying this reasoning to President Clinton's 1993 budget plan would begin by questioning each expenditure in terms of its purpose. Does it correct for some form of market failure? Does it improve income distribution? If not, it shouldn't be made. If yes, then the dollar value of the benefit(s) generated by the resources used in supporting this expenditure should be compared with the dollar benefit(s) those same resources would have produced in the private economy. Are the dollar benefits greater if the public sector spends those resources? If yes, proceed with the expenditure. How should those public dollars be raised? Taxes or borrowing? Which generations receive the benefits from the expenditure? If future generations receive benefits, then part of the expenditure should be financed through borrowing. If future generations are expected to be materially better-off than today's citizens, then part of this expenditure should be financed by borrowing. What about excess burden? If it can be reduced through borrowing, then again, part of this expenditure should be debt financed.

Obviously, given the mishmash of the politics that guides government expenditures, taxation, and borrowing, it would be senseless to think about Clinton's—or in fact, anyone else's—1993 budget in public finance terms. This simply reflects the fact that federal budgets are more of a political document than an economic game plan.

A SECOND BEST METHOD OF EVALUATING
PRESIDENT CLINTON'S 1993 FEDERAL BUDGET

Nevertheless, not all is lost. A second best method of evaluating any federal budget, including Clinton's 1993 one, is to ask of it the following two questions: Will society be materially better off (normally interpreted to mean more jobs in the economy) because of it? Will society have a fairer income distribution because of it?

One of the strongest motivating factors behind the president's 1993 budget package was to restore, what he perceived to be, a loss of fairness that occurred during the 1980s. During the presidential campaign of 1992 and after-wards, President Clinton emphasized how the "rich failed to pay their fair share of the tax burden" during the Reagan and Bush presidencies. The president's budget attempts to redress this by increasing the marginal tax rate on corporations and wealthy Americans. Before we analyze this policy change, let's look at the evidence behind his charge that the rich "got off easy" during the 1980s.

During the 1980s, the total effective federal tax rate (includes all federal taxes) on the middle 20 percent income bracket remained constant. For the top 1 percent of income earners it fell about 4 percent. From this perspective, the president is right. Looking at the share of *all* federal taxes paid, the middle's share fell during the 1980s by about 1 percent. The share of taxes paid by the top 1 percent rose by about 3 percent. From this viewpoint, the president is wrong.

Here also lies the rub in evaluating the president's budget as an income redistribution device. From a distance, it looks like the president's package of increasing tax rates on corporations and the wealthy will shift more of the federal tax burden away from the middle and poorer classes. This can be viewed as an improvement in income distribution. But up close, taking account of the effects these tax policy changes will have on job growth in the economy, a different result could emerge. To the extent that higher tax rates reduce the growth rates of corporations, jobs will be adversely effected. The same is true in increasing tax rates on wealthy Americans. What Congress discovered with its luxury tax (which was repealed in this budget package) is that it impacted the middle class more than the rich through loss of jobs. My conclusion, from all of this, is that the equity portion of the president's budget is more "smoke and mirrors" than substance; and in the long-run, might actually make the "average" individual worse off.

The predicted effect of Clinton's 1993 budget on jobs, which will determine whether in fact we are materially better-off, doesn't do much better than its income distribution half. The overall consensus among forecasters is that given its "carrots and sticks," the 1993 federal budget will have a slight drag on economic growth costing Americans hundreds of thousands of jobs. The biggest "stick" that will hit the economy will be increases in taxes that will cost the economy $241 billion. While there are many tax cuts in Clinton's budget, they are minuscule compared to the tax increases.

On the "carrot" side are lots of business tax incentives including extensions of the research tax credit, equipment write offs for small businesses, the creation of "empowerment zones" to encourage business investments in poor neighborhoods, etc. In addition, there are such "Turkish delights" as cuts in various agricultural programs, cuts in Medicare, cuts in welfare related to administrative costs, the reform of the student-loan program, cuts in housing assistance to those who don't qualify, and so forth.

Combining this with the possible failure of the budget to achieve an improvement in equity, spells an unsuccessful first effort on the part of the Clinton Administration. This conclusion is not surprising, however, given that the same probably could have been said about most presidential budgets in this century.

— 13 —

Bill Clinton:
The Post-Modern President

Steven Hayward

Out west in California, where the sun shines brightly all year round, the blue and red Clinton/Gore bumper strips were noticeably fading out by early spring on the thousands of cars whose owners were having trouble peeling them off. The quick fade-out seemed an omen for Clinton's spring collapse in the public opinion polls, which was even worse in California than nationally. By June, Rush Limbaugh was announcing the locations of body and fender shops who could remove the seemingly unremovable bumper strips, which had apparently been produced with sufficiently strong adhesive to last through two presidential campaigns.

California, remember, provided Clinton with one-third of his total national margin of victory in the popular vote, and is crucial to his prospects for re-election in 1996. California's rapid disenchantment with Clinton might be explained away as a function of frustration and impatience over the unyielding recession among a people that is unused to such prolonged economic doldrums. It is more likely that California, a high income state with a (once) thriving entrepreneurial culture, came quickly to grasp Clinton's innermost leftward character with the prompt announcement of his income tax hike.

California has seen this before, complete with the therapeutic New Age-speak about the "politics of meaning," under the regime of Jerry "Moonbeam" Brown. Brown, for all his kookiness of recent years, foreshadowed Clinton in one important respect: he was the first "New Democrat" who affected a moderate rhetoric while implementing hard left policies and appointing far-out lefties (like State Supreme Court Chief Justice Rose Bird). Hence, when Clinton lurched sharply to the left in the early weeks of his administration, Californians were able to see more quickly than others that Clinton had succeeded in winning the election by concealing who he is, and would attempt to govern in the same fashion.

It makes for revealing reading to go back to the references to Clinton in Peter Brown's ironically titled 1991 book *Minority Party: Why Democrats Face Defeat in 1992 and Beyond*. Clinton not only provided a warm dust jacket endorsement for the book, but is cited throughout on the need for the Democratic party to eschew the politics of class warfare and return to the political center. In hindsight the Brown book reads like a memorandum to Democrats on how to avoid another Dukakis debacle. All the themes of the 1992 campaign are articulated in Brown's book: the calculated public rebuke of Jesse Jackson, the embrace of the middle class, and the solicitude for the suburbs and heartland America. But the Clinton government—as opposed to the Clinton campaign—has betrayed most of this.

This was not, of course, how it was supposed to turn out. Clinton was supposed to be the culmination of the Democratic

Leadership Council effort to bring genuine moderation back to the Democratic party. In addition to Clinton's own proclamation that he is a "new kind of Democrat," it is worth noting that both the DLC's campaign tract *Mandate for Change* and even Vice President Gore's recent *Reinventing Government* initiative adopt the general tone of "the new paradigm" (for lack of a better term) of market forces, individual incentives, and leaner government institutions. Under the Clintonites, however, this prospective program of reform doesn't add up to limited government. At the core of the Clinton Project is the attempt to employ the rhetoric and perhaps even some of the ideas of limited government to serve liberal political ends.

It would be tempting to excuse Clinton by observing that, as the party of big government for nearly a century now, the prospect of moderation in the Democratic party was oversold from the beginning. In addition to the entrenched constituencies and the deep philosophical commitment to big government, there is the practical problem of personnel. Recalling the old adage that "personnel are policy," even without the perverted policy of "diversity" it is probably true that amongst the cadre of people available to staff a Democratic administration, there are no "New Democrats," or at least not enough.

What the character of the Clintonites shows is the deep imprint the 1960s has made on contemporary liberalism. This can be seen even among—or perhaps especially among—the young bucks like George Stephanopoulos who came of age after the 1960s, for whom it is axiomatic that the radical ferment of the 1960s represents the pinnacle of cultural enlightenment in America. It is not simply that the Clinton administration has extremely liberal ideas, as was belied by the Lani Guinier nomination. The entire tone of the Clintonites exudes a smug, post-modern certitude that intentions count for more than ideas, that they are morally superior because of their "caring" and "commitment." For such people, emoting is as good as analyzing.

Michael Oakeshott reminds us in his famous essay "On Being Conservative" that politics is an activity unsuited to the young. "Everybody's young days are a dream, a delightful insanity, a sweet solipsism," Oakeshott wrote. "Nothing in them has a fixed shape, nothing a fixed price; everything is a possibility, and we live happily on credit." A pretty good description, I think, of the youngsters on the White House staff. But it also accurately describes the older set in the White House; say, for instance, Al Gore. Not only has modern liberalism made the activist dreamer the stereotype of the modern politician, but the pervasive moral teaching of the 1960s has inhibited the baby boom generation from ever growing up, from ever acquiring the mature moral virtues necessary for responsible politics. This is noticeable in Clinton, who exhibits clear signs of arrested adolescence from time to time.

A vital aspect of Clinton's character, and the character of his politics, can be best understood by examining his close connection—some might call it an umbilical cord—to Hollywood. Much has been made of the direct role Hollywood producers such as the Bloodworth-Thomasons played in both the Clinton campaign and inauguration. But the Clinton-Hollywood connection goes deeper than the tactical advantages of Hollywood image-making. Clinton is plainly among the kind of politician who is drawn to politics partly as an alternative route to celebrity. Such people always have an affinity for the people who have achieved celebrity through the pre-eminent route of popular entertainment. Reagan's connection to Hollywood has obscured this phenomenon, because he related to Hollywood both as a professional peer and as a political dissident.

Liberal politicians like Clinton arrive in Hollywood as supplicants, not merely for money and endorsements, but for the moral approval the creative community supposedly confers. Clinton not only craves the approval of this segment of the "chattering class," but views Hollywood as a legitimate source of moral order. This can only mean trouble for America, as Hollywood has become (along with the universities) the principal repository of the residue of 1960s radicalism.

The Hollywood creative community (which should be understood to include popular music—"Don't Stop Thinking About Tomorrow"—as well as TV and movies) does indeed consider itself to be a major moral force. "Celebrities don't want to just be called to write checks," said Margery Tabankin, the executive director of the Hollywood Women's Political Committee and the head of the Barbra Streisand Foundation, told the *New York Times*. "Nobody in Hollywood comes to the table thinking that they have the answers on Bosnia. Come on! But they do come as artists, pained by human suffering, who want to bring their creative skills to the process." (This presumption explains much of Hollywood's fury at Vice President Quayle's famous Murphy Brown remark.)

In recent months Clinton has supposedly heeded the counsel of political advisers such as James Carville to tone down the visibility of his Hollywood connections. The first sign of trouble came with Maureen Dowd's front page story in the *New York Times* in May, which said that "the Clinton White House is extravagantly star-struck," and that things were "spinning out of control on the celebrity front." Dowd reported that Hollywood celebrities such as Barbra Streisand were being treated to policy briefings from cabinet members. (In an effort to burnish her credentials as a serious person, Streisand has declared herself to be a regular reader of *The Economist*, and several other Hollywood celebrities have even hired their own political consultants to advise them about politics.)

A superficial reticence toward Hollywood and the cultural elite would simply be of a piece with Clinton's general political shrewdness. But even with David Gergen around to restrain the impulses and spasms of the leftward core of Clintonism, the true character of Clinton's politics cannot be concealed or muted for very long. With Gergen around, gaffes like the Guinier nomination are less likely. ("To be Gergenized" wrote Michael Kelly of the *New York Times Magazine*, "is to be spun by the velveteen hum of this soothing man's smoothing voice into a state of such vertigo that the sense of what is real disappears into a blur." Precisely what Clinton requires if he is to succeed.) More often, the core of Clintonism will come to view in the form of post-modernism—the sort of preaching you see in Ms. Clinton's "politics of meaning" speech, or in Vice President Al Gore's book *Earth in the Balance*.

Ms. Clinton said that we must "redefine who we are as human beings in this post-modern age," which will require "remaking the American way of politics, government, indeed life." The idea of "redefining who we are in this post-modern age" implies that there is no human nature, or that whatever human nature there is defines itself through sheer self-assertion. In other words, the human soul can be transformed at will. So for Ms. Clinton to say that we need to remake the American way of politics, government, and life is to imply that government has the right, even the duty, to change man into something he now is not. She believes that this transformation can be achieved through proper administration. This captures the heart of what people glibly describe as "post-modernism;" it is the view that progress is no longer a material phenomenon, but a moral and spiritual phenomenon in an era that has eviscerated both morality and spirituality. (Hillary's "politics of meaning" speech served wonderfully for what the Clintonites like to call a "defining moment." Leon Wieseltier observed in *The New Republic* that "there is a certain sensibility, for which Mrs. Clinton's generation is famous, and which she perfectly exemplifies, that hates being preceded. Everything it experiences it experiences for the first time. When it sees, there is light; and when it fails to see, the whole world is covered in darkness.")

Vice President Gore similarly makes clear in *Earth in the Balance* that what is at stake in the environmental controversy is not merely the physical and economic calculations of natural resource use, or even the political institutions and incentives that govern the environment, but rather the spiritual quality of the human soul itself. For both the first lady's "politics of meaning" and the vice president's environmental ethic, to disagree on grounds of reason is to display a disorder of the soul. Like the premises of "political correctness" on the college campus, carried to its logical extreme this is the basis of tyranny. Oakeshott, again, reminds us that "the conjunction of dreaming and ruling generates tyranny."

It is probable that these tyrannical urges will be confined chiefly to rhetorical extravagances like the "politics of meaning" speech, chiefly because the actual policy ideas (such as worksite-based holistic therapists—an actual proposal of Hillary's guru Michael Lerner) remain inchoate or will not receive much enthusiasm in a Congress that is in the surprising position of finding itself to the right of the executive branch. The most serious political initiative of the Clintonites is, therefore, the crusade to revise public opinion about the 1980s.

We are told repeatedly that the prosperity of the 1980s was false, that only the rich got richer, and that economic ruin is just around the corner unless we raise taxes and enlarge the government. This tactic shows the seriousness of Clinton's political aims. It would be easy for him simply to attack George Bush and "the last four years," and let the more popular Reagan off lightly. Instead, Clinton is going after the entire decade, in a bold gambit to discredit the entire conservative philosophy of governing.[1] (In this crusade Clinton is receiving immense help from the news media. After presenting the facts about economic growth in the 1980s to a senior producer at ABC's "World News Tonight" recently in New York, the producer replied to me: "It can't be as you say. Everywhere we go and talk to the man on the street, people think the 1980s were bad.")

There is an eerie parallel to this revisionism. As readers of Thomas B. Silver's standout book *Coolidge and the Historians* will know, for two generations liberal historians have portrayed the prosperity of the 1920s as false and shallow, and favoring only the rich. The Republican leadership of the 1920s, especially Calvin Coolidge and Herbert Hoover, is portrayed as ignorant, inept, and mean. Henry Steele Commager, for instance, wrote that "the mark of failure is heavy on these years. . . . Rarely in our history have so many mediocrities been counterbalanced by so few men of talent." Other prominent historians like Arthur Schlesinger, Jr. made the case that the private sector, operating irresponsibly under ill-conceived low taxes and free market policies, caused the onset of the Great Depression.

None of this was true, as subsequent counter-revisionist historians have shown. Paul Johnson pointed out in his blockbuster *Modern Times* that the 1920s was one of the most fortunate decades in American history, with prosperity widely diffused. Johnson also points out, as has Milton Friedman and other economic historians, that it was the mistakes of *government*, not the private sector, that brought on and aggravated the Depression. And Silver's *Coolidge and the Historians* dispels the liberal slanders against Coolidge, and makes the case that Coolidge was one of the most intelligent and thoughtful leaders ever to occupy the White House.

Just as the denigration of the 1920s was a necessary part of the aggrandizement of the New Deal, today's revisionism of the 1980s is intended to aid the cause of a new phase of expanding the size and scope of government, which is why the Clinton administration is using the same playbook as the New Dealers, self-consciously citing the New Deal as its model and inspiration. The Clinton political program is an instant replay of the New Deal propaganda machine. This is why the new middle class entitlement of health care—rather than a welfare program for the underclass or minorities—is the centerpiece of the Clinton domestic agenda. The object of this revisionism is to cram Reagan and the 1980s down an Orwellian memory hole, and revive the old Democratic electoral coalition.

The real challenge of the opposition to Clintonism is to keep alive the Reaganite themes of limited government, low taxes, and deregulation. The good news is that the results of the 1993 off year election suggest that there is latent sentiment among voters for these themes. The test of the 1990s will be to see if the realignment in public sentiment that Reagan's victories helped to generate can be converted into a realignment of partisan preferences below the presidential level. Clinton's post-modern liberalism, if it can be effectively exposed, will be a powerful aid. This will not be as easy as it may have seemed in the spring of 1993, when Clinton was stumbling with every step. We should be chastened by the Bush campaign, which was merely a spectacular example of the routine Republican talent for snatching defeat from the jaws of victory. Clinton cannot be relied upon simply to be Jimmy Carter *redivivus*. We will have to make our own luck.

Endnote

1.   For a discussion of this issue see Mickey G. Craig, "Defending the Reagan Legacy: Rejecting Revisionist History," Ashbrook Essay number 7, Ashbrook Press, 1993.

— 14 —

Robert, Ross and Rush:
The State of the Opposition 1993

John J. Pitney, Jr.

As he ponders the opposition to his presidency, Mr. Clinton may sometimes wish the United States had a parliamentary system. National politics would focus on the floor of the Commons, where he could count on his party's support and where he could speak often and lengthily. Although several parties might have seats, only one would bear the official title of the loyal opposition. Political conflicts, however fierce, would have clear lines and workable dimensions.

President Clinton's life is not so simple. On the wide-open battleground of American politics, he has had to defend against many attackers, three of whom are named Robert Dole, Ross Perot, and Rush Limbaugh. These headstrong men do not work in tandem; indeed, Limbaugh often attacks Perot. But by fighting independently, they have already left the new administration with several years' worth of war wounds.

The president might seek consolation by remembering that even Franklin D. Roosevelt had to fend off armies of critics.

On closer look, the FDR comparison offers little comfort. In some ways, President Clinton's opponents pack more fire-power than the foes of the New Deal. And where FDR answered with coolness and skill, President Clinton has so far shown a thin skin, a tin ear, and only occasional flashes of the savvy that won him the White House.

Robert Dole

Why is Senate Republican Leader Robert Dole the real leader of the congressional opposition, instead of House Republican Leader Robert Michel? In the House, a simple majority can dictate the procedures for debate. If the Democrats enjoy a modest degree of unity, they can block votes on unfriendly amendments, waive points of order, and render the House GOP powerless on the floor. On the other side of the Capitol, the Senate's Rule XXII requires a three-fifths vote (sixty senators) to invoke cloture, that is, to stop debate. If Senator Dole and his forty-three GOP colleagues stick to-gether, they can sustain a filibuster and scuttle Clinton legis-lation. The president can seldom afford to ignore Senator Dole.

Senate minority leaders have not always had such power. At one point during FDR's tenure, Republicans had only seventeen seats, so they could not keep up a filibuster even though procedures of the time required a two-thirds vote for cloture. By the late 1970s, the Senate had adopted the current three-fifths rule—but Republicans had fewer than the forty-one seats needed to block cloture. The 1980 election suddenly gave them a majority, which they held until 1986. Although the next two elections held them above the forty-one-vote line, the ability to filibuster meant little: Republicans wanted to *pass* the programs of Reagan and Bush, not stall them. With the looming Clinton victory in 1992, forty-one again became the Republicans' magic number. On election night, they had forty-two. Soon afterwards, Paul Coverdell's win in a Georgia runoff brought them up to forty-three; and in June 1993, Kay Bailey Hutchison's landslide in a Texas special election boosted them to forty-four.

Moreover, they enjoyed more unity than in the past. From the New Deal through the 1970s, the Senate GOP included a sizable faction of liberals. Republicans such as Thomas Kuchel of California, who served as party whip until his loss in a 1968 primary, often supplied key votes for the programs of Democratic presidents. By 1992, retirements and defeats had thinned the liberals' ranks to the point where they no longer held a single leadership position.

In the spring of 1993, the Senate Republicans were poised for first blood. When President Clinton proposed his costly "economic stimulus" package, the GOP leadership got all Senate Republicans to sign a letter pledging a filibuster. They followed through, killing the bill and rattling the president.

The budget reconciliation bill, embodying President Clinton's economic program of major tax increases and modest spending restraints, offered the Senate GOP a different opportunity. Filibusters are forbidden on reconciliation bills, so the minority could not singlehandedly derail the Clinton plan—but its united opposition could force the Democrats to take all the blame for raising taxes. That way, Republicans could regain control of an issue that they had lost with the Darman budget deal of 1990. From a partisan standpoint, the outcome was perfect: because no Republican voted for the plan, and because it passed only when Vice President Gore broke a tie, every Democrat who voted aye could be charged with casting the decisive vote.

These fights did not have predestined results. Had President Clinton sought bipartisan support earlier in the year, he might have peeled off a few of the small band of liberal Republicans; luckily for Senator Dole, the president was so accustomed to the one-party Arkansas legislature that he was slow to grasp the importance of GOP support. Meanwhile, the Republican Leader used his backroom talents to hold potential defectors in check.

On other issues such as campaign finance, Senator Dole has had less success in maintaining the loyalty of liberal Republicans. Nevertheless, his power guarantees that the president must reckon with him—and that the news media will cover him. Always known for his caustic wit, he has been happy to lob well-timed sound bites at the Clinton White House. When the president's spokesman complained about GOP attacks, Senator Dole suggested that White House aides "calm down, go off for a weekend, have a Diet Coke."

In this respect, too, Senator Dole stands apart from most Republican congressional leaders of the past. Robert A. Taft of Ohio, the *de facto* GOP Senate leader during the 1940s, resembled Dole in several ways: he was a conservative Midwesterner with a retentive mind, a mastery of the legislative process, and an aura of *gravitas*. Unlike Dole, he did not leaven his seriousness with a sense of humor.

Other GOP leaders of the era were equally colorless without being equally intelligent, so they became easy targets for Democratic gibes. At a 1940 speech, FDR focused on three GOP lawmakers: Joseph Martin, Bruce Barton, and Hamilton Fish. He said that most people had supported his achievements—except "Martin, Barton, and Fish." He repeated the phrase throughout the speech, and soon the Madison Square Garden crowd was chanting it with him. Mr. Martin responded that the attack was "a bit unfair."

Perhaps President Clinton had that speech in mind when he needled Senator Dole at a White House correspondents dinner. But instead of making a deft joke, the president cracked that the economy-minded Kansan had sought millions of tax dollars for a Wichita boathouse. When that turned out to be false, the White House had to issue a meek apology. Not only did President Clinton look clumsy, but he had riled the owner of Washington's longest memory, sharpest mind, and most acerbic tongue.

With Senator Dole's aggressiveness in mind, some look forward to a Clinton-Dole presidential contest. Senator Dole might well be a formidable contender, but his candidacy would have three major problems.

First, despite his splendid legislative record, Senator Dole has had trouble in national campaigns. During the 1976 vice presidential debate, he referred to World War I and World War II as "Democrat wars," which enabled Democrats to portray him as a reckless hatchet man. In 1980, he finished seventh in the New Hampshire presidential primary, with 597 votes. Eight years later, after George Bush upset him in New Hampshire, he snapped at the winner: "Stop lying about my record." His 1988 campaign suffered not only from his attack-dog image but from internal chaos.

Second, he was born in 1923. Although he remains physically vigorous, he would have to fight the impression that he is out of step with the times. If the voters still want change, the Clinton reelection campaign might imply, why go back to the generation that passed the torch in 1992?

Third, he has yet to articulate an alternative to the Democratic agenda. In 1987, Senator Nancy Kassebaum said: "There's always a question: Does he have a vision?" She later apologized, but even his admirers acknowledge that he is more a legislative artisan than a visionary national leader.

ROSS PEROT

If Robert Dole equals Robert Taft plus humor, then Ross Perot equals Huey Long minus charm. Although many observers think that the Perot phenomenon is unprecedented, Long paved its populist way nearly sixty years ago. And just as the diminutive Texan constantly engages the attention of the Clinton White House, Long was a preoccupation of FDR. "It's all very well for us to laugh over Huey," Roosevelt warned his advisers. "But actually we have to remember all the time that he really is one of the two most dangerous men in the country." (Douglas MacArthur was the other.) As the Ross Perot of the New Deal era, Huey Long deserves a moment's attention.

After winning the Louisiana governorship in 1928, Long launched a massive program of social services and public works while gaining personal control of state government. In 1930, he won a seat in the Senate, where he became the leading spokesman for a radical program of wealth redistribution. Early in FDR's first term, he threatened a serious third-party challenge to the president's reelection. The challenge ended when he died in 1935.

Long had much in common with Perot:

• Though lacking great personal wealth, Long gathered a huge warchest from corporations doing business with Louisiana and state employees who had to kick back a fraction of their salaries. The "deduct box," as it was called, reportedly held a million dollars or more, an impressive sum for the mid-1930s.

• United We Stand America, Ross Perot's grassroots organization, has a clear forerunner in Long's 4.7 million-member network, called the Share Our Wealth Society. Like UWSA, Share Our Wealth could easily have served as the embryo for a national third party. During a half-hour radio broadcast in 1934 (shades of Perot's "infomercials"), Long called on Americans to form local chapters of his organization. His appeal could have served as a model for Perot: "Organize your share-our-wealth society and get your people to meet with you, and make known your wishes to your Senators and Representatives in Congress."

• Long wrote a policy manifesto in the form of a novel titled *My First Days in the White House*. The book promised sweeping cures for the country's ailments, which he blamed largely on the "Masters of Finance and Destiny." In a series of books, Perot has similarly demonized "domestic lobbyists, foreign lobbyists and representatives of political action committees."

• Long urged his listeners: "Save this country. Save mankind." Perot's latest book is titled *Save Your Job, Save Our Country*.

In spite of such parallels, there are also key differences. Long damned his critics as tools of special interests, but he did so for the sake of theatrical effect. Perot, by all accounts, really is prone to conspiracy theory and is hypersensitive to personal attacks. Long was an encyclopedic factmonger who could outdebate the wiliest advocates, whereas Perot gets flustered when he has to answer unexpected questions.

The most important difference lies in the reaction of each man's target. Franklin Roosevelt answered Long's challenge by addressing his policy concerns and invading his political base. In the Second Hundred Days—spanning the spring and summer of 1935—FDR got Congress to pass Social Security, tax reform and other measures that won over down-and-out voters who might have followed Long's call for radical change.

The Clinton forces have made some headway in dealing with Perot on a personal level. During a television debate on the North American Free Trade Agreement, Vice President Gore deliberately antagonized Perot with questions about his finances. Perot's petulant responses, including a preposterous denial that he had ever lobbied Congress, severely undercut his public standing and may have contributed to NAFTA's passage.

While the administration may have wounded Perot, it has not resolved the concerns of Perot supporters: wasteful government and insider politics. President Clinton's 1993 economic package sparked a hostile reaction because of the widespread belief that it raised taxes too much and cut spending too little. Vice President Gore's report on "Reinventing Government" briefly made the front pages but was rapidly eclipsed by overseas crises. The Clinton health plan got applause for its good intentions but groans for its incomprehensible details. And as the year wore on, the new administration produced its own crop of rumors, scandals and tales of infighting—the unmistakable earmarks of Washington insiders.

Even the NAFTA victory could backfire. To secure the agreement's passage, President Clinton cut side deals and promised to defend pro-NAFTA Republicans against campaign attacks. Inside Washington, these moves look like crafty leadership. Elsewhere, they look like pork-barrelling and bipartisan collusion. Whether or not Perot can engineer a personal comeback, the NAFTA vote could fuel anti-incumbency and foster third-party challenges to lawmakers of both parties.

RUSH LIMBAUGH

The power of Bob Dole and Ross Perot comes from familiar sources. Senator Dole holds a key institutional post where he can shape the laws, which in turn are upheld by the coercive power of the government. Ross Perot's influence hinges upon his wealth: without it, he would be just another opinionated customer at a Dallas barbershop. In the 1990s, says futurist Alvin Toffler, such traditional forms of power are giving way to another: the application of knowledge.

Enter Rush Limbaugh. This self-described "harmless little fuzzball" has neither a billion-dollar bank account nor a high office in Washington. What he *does* supply is more formidable: a daily barrage of facts and logic, delivered with wit and confidence.

Limbaugh is a multimedia master of the information age. In 1988, 260,000 people listened to Limbaugh on fifty-six radio stations. By 1993, Limbaugh's radio audience had grown to 17.9 million and the "Excellence In Broadcasting Network" included 622 stations. At the same time, his syndicated television program was winning a bigger audience share than "Arsenio Hall" and his newsletter was selling 353,000 copies a month. His first book had remained on the *New York Times* best-seller list for more than a year, and his second had a record-setting first printing.

Moreover, he knows that technology carries information in both directions, and members of his audience supply him with material via fax and computer e-mail.

What matters most is not the medium but the message. Limbaugh's broadcasts and writings carry out an essential task for any political opposition: hanging the establishment with its own words and deeds. He constantly searches the Clinton record for items that deserve the harsh light of reason and ridicule. His newsletter has published a lengthy and detailed catalog of broken promises and inconsistencies. On his television program, he contrasted President Clinton's Bosnia saber-rattling with his statement that we should not "get involved in a conflict in behalf of one of the sides." Limbaugh skewered the president's position with a simple question: Does this mean we're going to bomb *both* sides?

More recently, he juxtaposed a clip of candidate Bill Clinton ridiculing the "family values" issue with a clip of President Bill Clinton embracing the issue in a speech before religious leaders.

FDR never had to deal with the likes of Limbaugh. Will Rogers approximated Limbaugh's mix of humor and commentary, but he was on FDR's side. Some commentators have likened Limbaugh to Father Charles Coughlin, the infamous "radio priest" of the 1930s. This comparison is a smear. Father Coughlin preached a strange brew of statism, prejudice, and conspiracy theory. Limbaugh's message is about none of those things; rather it is about liberty, optimism, and a zest for verbal combat. Above all, it is about the joyful breaking of the taboos of "political correctness." In short, Rush Limbaugh is the morale officer of the Culture War.

President Clinton is uniquely vulnerable to the Limbaugh treatment. Not only does his administration supply Limbaugh with abundant ammunition, but he lets the gibes unnerve him. At the same correspondents dinner where he committed the Dole gaffe, Clinton mentioned a recent program in which Limbaugh had praised Attorney General Janet Reno for maintaining her composure when Representative John Conyers assailed her: "Did you like the way Rush stuck up for Janet Reno the other night on his program? He only did it because she was attacked by a black guy." This charge of racism diminished the president's stature while raising Limbaugh's: nothing so elevates an opposition leader as a personal attack from the president of the United States.

Others in the Clinton camp have also made intemperate criticisms. Rep. Dan Glickman of Kansas warned about Limbaugh's commentaries: "This lack of respect shown the president is worse than disgusting. It is also dangerous to the political integrity of this country." And Roger Clinton, one of the president's half-siblings, flatly called Limbaugh a "traitor" for daring to question the president's policies.

The most ominous reaction has come in the form of the "Hush Rush Bill." This pending legislation would restore the misnamed "Fairness Doctrine" to the regulation of the air-waves. Under the proposed rule, stations carrying Limbaugh's show and other controversial programming would have to "provide reasonable opportunity for the presentation of contrasting viewpoints"—or else risk serious challenge to their licenses. Because it is hard to define "reasonable opportunity," many stations might drop such programming rather than worry about costly litigation. In other words, lawmakers are considering the use of government to silence political opposition. The old form of power is trying to trump the new.

No mere jokester could prompt such a serious reaction. To President Clinton's congressional supporters, who know and fear the modern power of knowledge, Rush Limbaugh really is the most dangerous man in America.

Contributors

Peter W. Schramm is professor of political science and Associate Director of the Ashbrook Center, Ashland University, Ohio.

William A. Rusher is a columnist and Chairman of the Board of the John M. Ashbrook Center for Public Affairs, Ashland University.

Thomas B. Silver is chief of staff to Los Angeles County Supervisor Michael D. Antonovich.

David K. Nichols is associate professor of political science at Montclair State College, New Jersey.

John Zvesper is lecturer in politics at the University of East Anglia, England.

Fred Baumann is associate professor of political science at Kenyon College, Ohio.

Larry P. Arnn is President of The Claremont Institute, California.

Charles E. Parton is Director of the John M. Ashbrook Center for Public Affairs, Ashland University.

Patrick J. Garrity is a political scientist who has published widely on strategic affairs.

C. Bradley Thompson is assistant professor of political science and Coordinator for Special Programs of the Ashbrook Center, Ashland University.

Jeffrey J. Poelvoorde is associate professor of political science at Converse College, South Carolina.

Patrick B. McGuigan is chief editorial writer for *The Daily Oklahoman*, Oklahoma City, Oklahoma.

Mark A. Nadler holds the A.L. Garber Family Chair in Economics at Ashland University, Ohio.

Steven Hayward is research and editorial director for the Pacific Research Institute, a San Francisco-based think tank.

John J. Pitney, Jr. is assistant professor of government at Claremont McKenna College, California.

Selected Ashbrook Center Publications

Lessons of the Bush Defeat, ed. Peter W. Schramm (75 pp., paper, $3.00) 1993

Defending the Reagan Legacy: Rejecting Revisionist History, Mickey G. Craig (25 pp., paper, $3.00) 1993

Hope to the World for All Future Time: America and the World After the Cold War, David Tucker (25 pp., paper, $3.00) 1992

The Hamilton-Madison-Jefferson Triangle, Morton J. Frisch (39 pp., paper, $3.00) 1992

Suite 3505: The Story of the Draft Goldwater Movement, F. Clifton White (415 pp., cloth-$19.95, paper-$12.95) 1992

The Education of Teachers, Rita Kramer (16 pp., paper, $3.00) 1992

Why Are People Beating Up on Higher Education?, Chester Finn (22 pp., paper, $3.00) 1992

Illiberal Education: Political Correctness and the College Experience, Dinesh D'Sousa (19 pp., paper, $3.00) 1992

Academic Freedom, Lynne V. Cheney (30 pp., paper, $3.00) 1992

A "G.I. Bill for Children," Lamar Alexander (32 pp., paper, $3.00) 1992